Organic Olive Production Manual

TECHNICAL EDITOR
PAUL M. VOSSEN

PUBLICATION COORDINATORS
JERI OHMART AND DAVID CHANEY

FUNDING FOR THIS PUBLICATION PROVIDED BY THE CALIFORNIA DEPARTMENT OF FOOD AND AGRICULTURE BUY CALIFORNIA INITIATIVE AND TRUE NORTH FOUNDATION

University *of* **California**
Agriculture and Natural Resources

PUBLICATION 3505
2007

To order or obtain ANR publications and other products, visit the ANR Communication Services online catalog at http://anrcatalog.ucanr.edu/ or phone 1-800-994-8849. You can also place orders by mail or FAX, or request a printed catalog of our products from

University of California
Agriculture and Natural Resources
Communication Services
1301 S. 46th Street
Building 478 - MC 3580
Richmond, CA 94804-4600

Telephone 1-800-994-8849
510-665-2195
FAX 510-665-3427
E-mail: anrcatalog@ucanr.edu

Publication 3505

ISBN-13: 978-1-60107-440-9

Library of Congress Control Number: 2006910294

Photo credits are given in the acknowledgments. Cover photo by Alexandra Kicenik Devarenne. Design by Will Suckow.

UC PEER REVIEWED This publication has been anonymously peer reviewed for technical accuracy by University of California scientists and other qualified professionals. This review process was managed by ANR Associate Editor for Pomology, Viticulture, and Subtropical Horticulture.

POD-11/15-SB/WFS

CONTENTS

PREFACE AND ACKNOWLEDGMENTS

This *Organic Olive Production Manual* provides detailed information for growers on how to produce olives organically. It addresses production issues, economics, pest control, the conversion process, and organic certification and registration. This manual has been developed as a supplement to the *Olive Production Manual, Second Edition*, which was published by the University of California Agriculture and Natural Resources in 2005 (Publication 3353). Organic growers are advised to consult both publications as they develop and refine their production systems.

The *Olive Production Manual, Second Edition*, is a comprehensive resource for commercial growers, from orchard planning and maintenance to harvesting and postharvest processing, and it provides information that is applicable to both organic and conventional productions systems. The manual contains new and expanded information on pollination, pruning for shaker and vertical rotating comb harvest, mechanical pruning, deficit irrigation, mechanical harvesting methods including trunk-shaking and canopy contact harvesters, postharvest handling and processing methods, and olive oil production. It also addresses management of olive fly, oleander scale, olive mite, and black vine weevil.

Funding for this project was provided by the Buy California Initiative, the California Department of Food and Agriculture, and the U.S. Department of Agriculture. The content of this publication does not necessarily reflect the views or policies of CDFA or USDA, nor does any mention of trade names, commercial products, and organizations imply endorsement of them by CDFA or USDA. We also acknowledge support from the True North Foundation for this project, which included a series of workshops on organic production. Most of the material in this publication is based on presentations given at the Organic Olive Production Workshop held May 27, 2005, in Santa Rosa. The authors would like to thank Jeri Ohmart and David Chaney of the University of California Sustainable Agriculture Research and Education Program for their assistance in organizing the workshop and for coordinating the many tasks involved in seeing this manual through to publication.

··

PHOTO CREDITS

Jack Kelly Clark: plates 6.1, 6.2, 7.1, 7.4, 7.7, 7.8. Joseph H. Connell: plates 1.1, 5.2, 5.4, 5.5. Jeffrey A. Creque: plates 9.1, 9.2. Alexandra Kicenik Devarenne: plates 6.3, 6.4, 6.5, 6.6, 6.7, 6.9. Stephen R. Gliessman: plates 10.2, 10.3. Ali Khatibi: plate 9.3. Paul M. Vossen: plates 1.2, 1.3, 1.4, 1.5, 2.1, 3.1, 3.2, 3.3, 3.4, 5.1, 5.3, 5.6, 5.7, 6.8, 7.2, 7.3, 7.5, 7.6, 8.1, 8.2, 8.3, 8.4, 8.5, 8.6, 10.1, 10.4.

AUTHORS

TECHNICAL EDITOR

PAUL M. VOSSEN, University of California Cooperative Extension, Sonoma and Marin Counties

CONTRIBUTING AUTHORS

DAVID CHANEY, University of California Sustainable Agriculture Research and Education Program

JOSEPH H. CONNELL, University of California Cooperative Extension, Butte County

JEFFREY A. CREQUE, McEvoy Ranch, Land Stewardship Consultant

STEPHEN R. GLIESSMAN, University of California, Santa Cruz, Department of Environmental Studies

RAY GREEN, California Department of Food and Agriculture Organic Program

ALEXANDRA KICENIK DEVARENNE, University of California Cooperative Extension, Sonoma County

WILLIAM H. KRUEGER, University of California Cooperative Extension, Glenn County

W. THOMAS LANINI, University of California, Davis, Department of Plant Sciences

L. ANN THRUPP, Fetzer Vineyards and California Sustainable Winegrowing Alliance

PAUL M. VOSSEN, University of California Cooperative Extension, Sonoma and Marin Counties

PUBLICATION COORDINATORS

JERI OHMART, University of California Sustainable Agriculture Research and Education Program

DAVID CHANEY, University of California Sustainable Agriculture Research and Education Program

AUTHORS

TECHNICAL EDITOR

PAUL M. VOSSEN, University of California Cooperative Extension, Sonoma and Marin Counties

CONTRIBUTING AUTHORS

DAVID CHANEY, University of California Sustainable Agriculture Research and Education Program

JOSEPH H. CONNELL, University of California Cooperative Extension, Butte County

JEFFREY A. CREQUE, McEvoy Ranch, Land Stewardship Consultant

STEPHEN R. GLIESSMAN, University of California, Santa Cruz, Department of Environmental Studies

RAY GREEN, California Department of Food and Agriculture Organic Program

ALEXANDRA KICENIK DEVARENNE, University of California Cooperative Extension, Sonoma County

WILLIAM H. KRUEGER, University of California Cooperative Extension, Glenn County

W. THOMAS LANINI, University of California, Davis, Department of Plant Sciences

L. ANN THRUPP, Fetzer Vineyards and California Sustainable Winegrowing Alliance

PAUL M. VOSSEN, University of California Cooperative Extension, Sonoma and Marin Counties

PUBLICATION COORDINATORS

JERI OHMART, University of California Sustainable Agriculture Research and Education Program

DAVID CHANEY, University of California Sustainable Agriculture Research and Education Program

Part 1
Site, Varieties, and Economics of Organic Olive Production

1

Site, Varieties, and Production Systems for Organic Olives

PAUL M. VOSSEN

INTRODUCTION

Demand by consumers for organically grown foods has been increasing steadily, and there is certainly an interest in olive oil and table olives produced from organically grown olives. Extra virgin olive oil and pickled olives are considered health foods made with very old natural processes that are inherently good and positive. Some consumers buy organic olive oil to avoid the potential contamination from chemicals used in conventional farming; others are motivated primarily by a desire to keep conventional pesticides out of the environment. In certain situations olives can contain residues from chemicals that have been applied to control insect pests or foliar diseases. Fortunately, these situations are not common, because olives have very few pest problems that require synthetic chemicals, and in almost all cases, there are alternative organic materials or procedures. Even though olives are easy to grow organically, it costs more to produce a bottle of olive oil or a jar of table olives using organic production methods. Yields can be lower, costs can be higher, and there is more risk for the producer. Like any other agricultural enterprise, organic olive production needs to be profitable. If some consumers are willing to pay more for it or choose it over another product, "organically grown" becomes a quality factor (sidebar 1.1).

Fortunately, olives are easily grown organically with few problems compared to some other agricultural crops. Many cultural practices and pest control methods available to olive growers qualify as USDA certifiably organic. An organic olive grower must, however, seek every possible advantage in the establishment phase of an orchard to minimize production difficulties and maximize production efficiency. An olive grower in business to make a profit using growing methods that do not harm the environment or contaminate the product is performing a good service and deserves a higher price. That advantage is diminished if yields are low, the trees take too long to come into bearing, quality is not excellent, or production costs are excessively high. Therefore the decisions made in

---

Sidebar 1.1

Conventional versus organic olive production

One study (Vossen et al. 2005) gives the following costs for organic and conventional production:

Conventional
- Easier weed control (herbicide: $15/acre)
- Easier fertility management (nitrogen: $102/acre)
- Easier scale control
- Possible residue problem
- Negative public perception
- Easier to get high yield

Organic
- Expensive weed control (weed cloth: $1,400/acre)
- Expensive fertility (compost and cover crop: $350/acre)
- Difficult scale control
- No pesticide residues
- Positive public perception
- Possible higher value
- High yield is more difficult or more expensive

site selection, site preparation, choice of varieties, tree spacing, tree training, irrigation management, pest control, and harvest method become critical. If all of those choices are correct for the situation, there is a better chance of making a profit and sustaining the business.

The ability of land to produce consistently high yields of excellent-quality olives either for table fruit or oil can vary considerably. Some soils and locations can produce excess vigor, while others require more management and inputs to induce adequate vigor. Resident perennial weeds, steep terrain, poor drainage, rocks, frost, wind, rainy conditions during bloom or harvest, and a multitude of other conditions can make olive growing considerably more expensive or impossible than in sites without those problems.

Harvest costs have typically amounted to half of the total production cost for olives. Therefore, the most important choice for a new olive orchard, beyond site location, is to select the best method for harvest. Subsequent decisions of variety choice, tree spacing, training method, and the rest of the production system fall into place more or less simultaneously. Harvesting little marbles from a large tree can be very expensive, especially if they are immature green and are not ready to come off. Mechanical methods exist, but they are not adequately effective for table olives without removal problems associated with tree form and fruit bruising. Over-the-row harvesters and trunk shakers for oil olive harvest are still relatively new in California and add complexity to the whole system relative to site selection, varieties, spacing, tree training, pruning, and pest control. For more information on harvest methods, see chapter 20, "The Olive Harvest," in the *Olive Production Manual, Second Edition.*

There is more flexibility in the choice of an olive orchard site when the fruit is grown for oil production than when it is grown for table fruit. The primary differences are the lack of importance of large fruit size, the greater tolerance for fruit damage from olive fruit fly, and more options for mechanical harvest. Less irrigation water is needed for oil olives than for table fruit because of the sizing issue, but table olives may be able to be grown on steeper terrain when hand-harvested compared with what is needed to accommodate large, top-heavy over-the-row machines. Hot areas with better soils and plenty of irrigation water would be much better for table fruit growers than for oil producers. That does not mean that oil producers can neglect fruit fly, excessively damage the fruit during harvest, or neglect irrigation, but those things are just not quite as critical as they are for table olive growers.

Olive trees are tough and can survive conditions that would kill most other plants, giving us the impression that olive trees can be grown without irrigation on rocky hillsides. However, those poor conditions that appear romantic while on vacation in Southern Europe, North Africa, or the Middle East have nothing to do with economic success here in California. Many dry-farmed orchards growing on steep rocky terrain took many, many years to reach their full production, which is only a fraction of what an irrigated orchard in better soil could achieve years earlier. Those orchards exist because olives will survive and produce something on such sites, while the deep soils in the valleys are saved for vegetables, berries, and other more demanding types of fruit trees. The reality of most olive production in the countries surrounding the Mediterranean is that they are marginal orchards producing marginal yields with marginal returns. Many producers keep going only on government subsidies, and in fact, many of the less-productive orchards have been abandoned. In some cases, orchardists with poor production have sought to sell an ecological (organic) product in hopes of offsetting their lower volume with higher prices (plate 1.1).

SITE SELECTION AND PREPARATION

When looking at the feasibility of a piece of ground for olive production, attention must be paid to climate, slope, soil type, drainage, rooting depth, and irrigation water.

Climate

The climatic conditions best for olives include mild winter temperatures that seldom get much below freezing. Young olive trees and branches on older trees can be killed at temperatures below about 22°F (–5.5°C), and fruit is damaged at temperatures below about 29°F (–1.7°C) (sidebar 1.2). These temperatures are not exact, because the effects of temperature vary according to the temperature measured at the ground

---

Sidebar 1.2
Damaging climatic conditions for olives

- Winter: Young trees damaged at < 25°F (–4°C)
- Winter: Small branches of mature trees damaged at < 22°F (–5.5°C)
- Winter: Mature trees killed at <15°F (–9.5°C)
- Autumn: Fruit before harvest damaged at < 29°F (–1.7°C)
- Spring: Rain, very high humidity, or hot dry wind at bloom

level around the trees, the duration of the low temperature, olive variety, tree age, and whether the trees have had a chance to harden off. In locations above 2,000 feet (610 m) elevation, in frost pockets, or more northerly sites where winter cold is a concern, olive trees should be deficit-irrigated in the autumn, and nitrogen fertilization should be limited, so the trees will not be flush with succulent growth entering the winter.

Even selecting the most cold-hardy varieties and hardening off the trees before winter helps protect trees only by a few degrees Fahrenheit. It is best to completely avoid planting olives in situations where there is a high risk of frost (temperatures below 32°F, or 0°C) during bloom (late April to mid-May) or where freezing temperatures are likely before harvest. Table fruit is usually harvested in October in California, but oil olives are often left until mid-December and sometimes into late January. If the likelihood of freezing temperatures at a particular site are high and those situations occur frequently or for extended periods through the day (instead of light nocturnal freezes), that site is unsuitable for olive production. Though not damaging to trees from a temperature standpoint, heavy, wet snow can break branches in olive trees. Olives do require some chilling (vernalization); about 200 hours below 45°F (7.2°C) is needed to induce proper bloom. This is not a problem in California's Mediterranean climate. Areas with hot, dry winds or rain during bloom should also be avoided in order to better assure good fruit set. For information on the hardiness and sensitivity of varieties to cold, see table 1.1.

Slope

Steep slopes significantly increase the cost of all cultural operations, especially harvest and fruit transport. For safety reasons, slopes that are too steep for tractor work or travel in an all-terrain-vehicle (ATV) should be avoided. In most cases, steep ground should not be cultivated because of the increased threat of soil erosion. Cover crops can help control erosion in nontilled orchards, but more irrigation water is needed to offset use by the cover crop.

Soil

Soils should be evaluated for internal drainage, surface drainage, rooting depth, layering, and mineral content. The ideal soil for olives is very well drained and deep enough to allow for internal drainage and to avoid saturated soil conditions. One of the few things that will kill and severely limit the growth of olives is heavy, wet, poorly drained soil conditions. Soils

---

Sidebar 1.3
Soil chemical properties that sustain adequate growth in olives

The values below are given for saturated paste extract. Mineral levels outside these values could lead to growth problems. Spending a lot of money to create ideal soil conditions does not generally prove to be cost-effective for olives, although nitrogen is often added after planting.

- High magnesium: < 1:1 ratio with calcium
- High calcium: > 8:1 ratio with magnesium
- Adequate phosphorus: > 10 ppm phosphorus
- Adequate potassium: > 125 ppm potassium
- High boron: > 2 ppm boron
- High chloride: > 10–15 meq/l chloride
- High sodium: SAR > 15
- Soil pH: 5.0–8.5

---

with clay, sand, hardpan, or gravel layers should be avoided or modified with a backhoe or trencher prior to planting. Some soils can be improved by installing subsurface drain lines and by improving surface drainage by planting trees on raised berms. Shallow soils can be used for olives as long as there is some slope to carry away excess winter rainwater, internal drainage is good, and there is adequate irrigation water available to offset what would normally be stored in a deeper soil. Producers in Mediterranean climates have demonstrated that olives can be grown in soil types ranging from gravel to sand to loam, but rarely in pure clay.

The pH tolerance of olives is quite large, ranging from about 5 to 8.5; ideally it would be adjusted to approximately 6.5, but it has not been demonstrated to be cost-effective to spend exorbitantly to develop an ideal pH. Nor has it been economically worthwhile in most cases to add phosphorus (P) or calcium (Ca) to soils, since these nutrients are normally in abundance; the exception would be for serpentine soils that are excessively high in magnesium (Mg). Toxic levels of sodium (Na), boron (B), or other minor elements are not common but have been observed in California. Potassium (K) may be needed for olives, and it can be added prior to planting. Nitrogen is almost always added after planting (sidebar 1.3).

New growing sites should be measured for rooting depth. This is commonly done with a backhoe that can rapidly dig test holes for observation. Holes should be dug at the drip line of any existing trees on the property. The cut surface should be observed for the presence of roots, which will reveal whether conditions are acceptable for growth. Prior to planting, the soil should be tested for at least sodium, magnesium, calcium, potassium, and pH. If there is a question about the history of the soil, existing vegetation shows odd symptoms or poor growth, or other soils in the area have known toxic levels of excess minor nutrients, then more tests are justified. Multiple subsamples should be taken from at least two depths within the root zone at about 6 inches and 18 inches (15 and 46 cm) for each observable soil type on the farm. Do not rely on analysis of soil samples from a home soil testing kit. Several reputable labs are listed in various UC Web sites, such as the list from the Sonoma County Cooperative Extension Web site, http://cesonoma .ucdavis.edu/vitic/pdf/commercial_labs_05.pdf.

Contact your local UC Cooperative Extension Farm Advisor for a nonbiased evaluation of your soil test results. Beware of exaggerated yield or plant health claims by fertilizer or compost salespeople.

Deep, fertile soils that lead to above-standard growth and production in other orchard crops actually lead to reduced growth and production in olives. In deep, fertile soils, olives tend to produce excessive vegetative growth, becoming too tall and producing little fruit. When excess shoot growth is pruned to keep olive trees smaller, they respond by sending out long, vigorous, nonfruitful shoots in most cases. Olive trees tend to fruit better under conditions of low vigor, including minimal nutrition, as long as there are no deficiencies.

Irrigation

Olive trees respond amazingly well to adequate irrigation water. They produce good growth, large fruit size, annual bearing, and much better yields than inadequately watered or highly water-stressed trees. Sites need to be evaluated to determine whether there is adequate volume and quality of irrigation water available to make the orchard economically competitive.

The minimum amount of irrigation water generally needed for good production in California is about 7,000 gallons per acre (65.5 m³/ha) per day, or a continuous 5 gallons (18.9 l) per minute. Cool coastal areas may be able to get by with less, and hot interior valleys may need more; table fruit producers may also need more to assure good fruit size. This minimum amount is based on providing adequate water to trees during the peak need periods of June through September. Recent irrigation trials with olives indicate that water can be reduced with a controlled deficit strategy, applying about 45 percent of total evapotranspiration demand from June until mid-August without affecting yield or fruit size in table olives (Berenguer et al. 2006; Grattan et al. 2006). Controlled deficit irrigation can be extended right up to harvest in oil olive orchards since fruit size is of little concern. For oil olives, fruit

---

Sidebar 1.4
Site selection: Olive irrigation requirements

Olives need 1 to 2 acre feet per year (1,233 to 2,466 m³/yr) of water, or 325,000 to 650,000 gallons (3,042 to 6,084 m³), applied at a minimum rate of 3 to 5 gallons per minute (11.4 to 19 l/min). Avoid water containing:

- High boron: > 1 to 2 mg/l, 2 ppm
- Bicarbonate: 3.5 ppm
- Total salt: > 3.0 dS/m EC, 480 ppm
- High sodium: > 3 meq/l, 9 SAR
- High chloride: 345 ppm

---

water content below about 48 percent leads to better extraction, stronger-flavored oils, and oils with better keeping qualities. Non-water-deficit conditions are very important for all olives from bloom to pit hardening to assure size and adequate growth for next year's crop. Table fruit also requires nondeficit conditions from mid-August to harvest to avoid fruit sizing problems.

In order to get young trees off to a good start and to fill their allotted space in the orchard as quickly as possible (which means rapid fruiting and a good return on investment), the trees should never be allowed to go dry and should never suffer any water stress. This means that young trees need frequent irrigations. With drip irrigation this means watering the trees every day or at least every other day during the heat of the summer (sidebar 1.4).

The total needs of olive trees can be calculated based on historical climatic demand, which can be determined by getting evapotranspiration data from weather stations on the Internet at http://wwwcimis .water.ca.gov/cimis/welcome.jsp. Coastal areas range from a total seasonal need of about 12 inches (30.5 cm), or about 325,000 gallons per acre (3,042 m³/ha) per year, for oil production, whereas table fruit in most California Central Valley locations requires about 36 inches (91 cm), or about 1 million gallons per acre (9,360 m³/ha) per year. The amount of water needed for irrigation is based on the climatic demand of the growing site after subtracting the amount of water stored in the soil from winter rainfall. The general rule of thumb is that most soils hold about 2 inches (5 cm) of available water per foot of rooting depth; sand holds less and clay more. Knowing the soil type and rooting depth can then help determine water needs, irrigation timing, and application rates.

Irrigation water quality is important for olives. Water should be tested for pH, electro-conductivity (EC), sodium, bicarbonate (HCO_3), sodium absorption ratio (SAR), chloride, boron, nitrate (NO_3), or any other suspected regional problem materials. Levels of boron should be below 1 to 2 mg/l, EC should be lower than 3.0 dS/m, bicarbonate below 3.5 meq/l, and sodium less than 3 meq/l (see sidebar 1.4). Help with evaluation of water analysis test results is available from UC Cooperative Extension Farm Advisors.

....

OLIVE VARIETIES

- **Manzanillo** (Manzanilla de Sevilla) is the most widely planted table variety in California and the world. It is highly productive, with uniform fruit size, and is more easily managed than most other varieties. It has relatively high oil content and produces excellent oil. Its disadvantages are lower cold hardiness and greater susceptibility to olive knot and Verticillium wilt than some other table varieties.

- **Sevillano** (Gordal Sevillana) is the second most widely planted table variety in California. It produces very large fruit with very high water content and very low oil content, though the oil quality is interesting and unique. It is more cold hardy and more resistant to olive leaf spot than most other table varieties, but the most attractive to olive fruit fly.

- **Mission** is a unique variety probably developed as a seedling selection and introduced into California by the Mission padres. It is a dual-purpose variety with good fruit size and high oil content. Trees grow very upright and are more cold hardy than many other varieties, but they are very susceptible to the foliar disease peacock spot. Oil quality can be excellent if the fruit is harvested at an appropriate maturity level.

- **Ascolano** (Ascolana) is a large-fruited variety with a soft texture, low oil content, and limited demand as a table fruit. It produces excellent oil that is quite unique in character. The trees are more cold hardy and resistant to peacock spot and olive knot than most other varieties.

- **Kalamata** (Kalamon) is a well-known variety with a characteristic size and shape. Its adaptability to California conditions is not known.

Pickled table olives can be made from any variety and it is common to see different specialty olives sold in each little village around the Mediterranean. Excellent quality, however, is normally based on large size, ease of pit removal, flesh to pit ratio, and texture after processing.

Most olive cultivars range in oil content from 10 to 30 percent of their fresh weight at full maturity. Of the major olive cultivars grown in California, Manzanillo (averaging 68 percent of California's production), Sevillano (15 percent), Ascolano (10 percent), and Mission (5 percent), only Mission contains a high enough oil content to plant specifically for oil. Varieties with an average oil yield of less than 20 percent, approximately 40 to 45 gallons of oil per fresh ton (167 to 188 l/T) of fruit, are not usually profitable to use for oil. Early-harvest table olives typically yield less than 20 gallons of oil per ton (83.5 l/T). Oil quantity and quality are highly dependent on the variety. The best oil varieties in the world have developed their reputations over centuries of production for fruit yields, oil content, flavor, keeping quality, maturity date, and ease of harvest. Table 1.1 gives selected information on primary olive cultivars.

Thousands of oil varieties exist, most of which are confined to small regional areas. Many of these varieties along with their traditional pollinizer and blending varieties have been introduced into California in the past few years. Regional adaptability of these oil varieties in California is not known. In fact, little is known worldwide regarding performance of different varieties outside their traditional growing regions. What many California growers have done is match their variety choices with similar Mediterranean climatic regions. Market popularity and the flavor appeal of their favorite oils are also major factors.

Proper selection of pollinizer varieties that are known to improve set in the main varieties is important to assure adequate cross-pollination. Since olives are wind-pollinated, pollinizers should be placed within 200 feet (61 m) of the main variety and preferably upwind (see table 1.1 for various cultivars and their qualities).

Plate 1.2 shows several olive varieties that were picked on the same day.

Flavor

The flavor components of each cultivar come from the water-soluble flavonoids, phenols, polyphenols, tocopherols, and esters that make up the bitter flavor of fresh olives. These compounds are naturally occurring antioxidants that extend shelf life of oil by reducing rancidity, and they are also the source of the fruity character of the oil. Oils with a high content of

Table 1.1. Primary olive cultivars

Cultivar	% oil	Cold hardiness	Fruit size	Polyphenol content*	Pollinizer varieties†
Arbequina	22–27	hardy	small	low	self-compatible
Arbosana	23–27	hardy	small	medium-high	Arbequina, Koroneiki
Aglandau	23–27	hardy	medium	medium	self-compatible
Ascolano	15–22	hardy	large	medium	Manzanillo, Mission
Barnea	16–26	sensitive	medium	medium	self-compatible, Manzanillo, Picholine
Barouni‡	13–18	hardy	large	medium	Manzanillo, Ascolano, Mission
Bosana	18–28	hardy	medium	high	Tondo de Cagliari, Pizzé Carroga
Bouteillan	20–25	hardy	medium	medium	Aglandau, Melanger Verdale
Chemlali	26–28	hardy	very small	high	self-compatible
Coratina	23–27	sensitive	medium	very high	self-compatible, Cellina di Nardo, Ogliarola
Cornicabra	23–27	hardy	medium	very high	self-compatible
Empeltre	18–25	sensitive	medium	medium	self-compatible
Farga	23–27	hardy	medium	medium	Arbequina
Frantoio	23–26	sensitive	medium	medium-high	Pendolino, Moraiolo, Leccino
Hojiblanca	18–26	hardy	large	medium	self-compatible
Kalamon	15–25	moderate	large	medium	Koroneiki, Mastoides
Koroneiki	24–28	sensitive	very small	very high	Mastoides
Leccino	22–27	hardy	medium	medium	Frantoio, Pendolino, Moraiolo
Manzanillo§	15–26	sensitive	large	high	Sevillano, Ascolano
Maurino	20–25	hardy	medium	high	Lazzero, Grappolo
Mission§	19–24	hardy	medium	high	Sevillano, Ascolano
Moraiolo	18–28	sensitive	small	very high	Pendolino, Maurino
Pendolino	20–25	hardy	medium	medium	Moraiolo, Frantoio, Leccino
Picholine	22–25	moderate	medium	high	self-compatible, Aglandau
Picual	24–27	hardy	medium	very high	self-compatible, Picudo
Picudo	22–24	hardy	large	low	Hojiblanca, Picual, Ocal
Sevillano‡	12–17	hardy	very large	low	Manzanillo, Mission, Ascolano
Taggiasca	22–27	sensitive	medium	low	self-compatible

Notes:

* Oils with a high polyphenol content have a longer shelf life and are generally more bitter and pungent.

† Most olive varieties are somewhat self-incompatible. They will usually set a better crop with cross-pollination, especially under adverse weather conditions. Leccino, Pendolino, Moraiolo, and Maurino are self-sterile and require a pollen source from another variety.

‡ Barouni and Sevillano are not compatible cross-pollinizers for each other.

§ Manzanillo and Mission are not compatible cross-pollinizers for each other.

Table 1.2. General description of the flavor of oil from selected olive cultivars

Mild	Medium	Strong
Arbequina	Aglandau	Arbosana
Ascolana	Barnea	Chemlali
Empeltre	Bosana	Coratina
Kalamon	Bouteillan	Cornicabra
Leccino	Farga	Frantoio
Maurino	Hojiblanca	Koroneiki
Pendolino	Manzanillo	Moraiolo
Picudo	Mission	Picholine
Sevillano		Picual
Taggiasca		

Table 1.3. Intensity of sensory characteristics of single-variety Tuscan olive oils

Variety	Fruity	Green	Bitter	Pungent	Sweet
Frantoio	****	**	**	****	**
Leccino	***	*	*	**	*****
Maurino	****	**	**	***	****
Moraiolo	****	**	****	***	**
Pendolino	****	*	***	**	***

Source: Cimato et al. 1995.

Note: Each asterisk indicates an increase in intensity.

polyphenol have a long shelf life (up to 2 years), are somewhat bitter when first made, and can cause a temporary burning sensation in the back of the throat when swallowed. Oils with short shelf lives (about 1 year) may be very fruity when first made, but their flavor diminishes and they turn rancid quickly.

Single-varietal oils are usually not as complex as blended oils and may not possess a balance of fragrance, full-bodied flavor, and complexity. Blending offers the opportunity to mask astringency, add longevity to low-polyphenol oil, and create depth.

European Varieties

The primary variety grown in Southern Italy is Coratina, which is a very late-maturing fruit that has a very high polyphenol content. It produces regular crops and is easily managed but is cold sensitive. Another very popular variety from Italy is Frantoio, which is somewhat cold sensitive and produces a strongly pungent and herbaceous fruity oil. Leccino is a popular cold hardy Italian variety that comes into bearing early and has a milder oil used mostly for blending. The most widely grown oil variety in the world is Picual, from Southern Spain. This variety comes into bearing early, has very high oil content, and is easily harvested with trunk shakers. Overripe Picual produces a characteristic oil flavor. Arbequina, from Northern Spain, is the most widely planted oil variety in the world right now. It is quite cold hardy, comes into bearing early, produces oil that is very fruity but not bitter or pungent, and forms the basis for the super-high-density production system. Koroneiki is a very productive Greek variety that produces oil with a strong and distinctive flavor. It is somewhat cold sensitive and produces very small fruit that are economically harvestable only with an over-the-row mechanical harvester.

Table 1.3 shows an example of the differences in sensory characteristics from single-varietal oils produced in Tuscany, Italy. The two strongest influences on the style of oil produced are the variety and ripeness of the fruit at harvest. The moisture content of the fruit from irrigation or rainfall, fruit handling procedures, and processing system also can influence the ultimate flavor of the oil. Most producers compose their oils for specific market segments by blending different lots of oils produced from distinct varieties that have been harvested at preselected fruit maturities.

TREE SPACING AND PRODUCTION SYSTEMS

The traditional spacing of more than 30 feet (7 m) between trees is no longer popular anywhere in the world except for desert dry-farmed areas. Modern olive oil trees are planted either at a high-density of about 200 to 350 trees per acre (494 to 865 per ha) or a super-high-density of 600 to 900 trees per acre (1,482 to 2,223 per ha). The high-density hedgerow system (200 to 350 trees per acre) is primarily used to accommodate specific varieties, achieve an aesthetic look with larger trees, and in situations where the ground is too steep or farms are too small to accommodate over-the-row mechanical harvesting (plate 1.3). The more trees planted per acre, the faster the planting comes into bearing; but as we only have a short experience with the super-high-density system, the long-term performance is not known.

Any variety can be grown with the high-density system because inputs are much less critical and cultural practices are not as exacting. The super-high-density system, however, has worked with only three varieties: Arbequina, Arbosana, and Koroneiki. Any other variety spaced closer than about 20 feet (6 m) apart may have excellent results the first few years, but the trees eventually tend to get too big for their amount of allotted space, grow too tall, and shade the lower portions of the tree. One way to get more trees per acre early is to plant them in a hedgerow configuration in a north–south orientation with less space between trees compared to between rows. Common spacings in this configuration range from 8 by 16 feet to 10 by 20 feet (2.4 by 4.9 m to 3.0 by 6.0 m). Shading in closely spaced orchards greatly reduces production. If the trees eventually grow too close together, alternate trees can be removed to reduce shading. Trying to keep most olive tree varieties small with hard pruning results in vigorous shoot growth and poor production.

The super-high-density system never allows the trees to exceed a size of about 9 to 10 feet tall by 6 to 7 feet wide (2.7 to 3.0 m by 1.8 to 2.1 m) through annual renewal pruning (plate 1.4 and sidebar 1.5). The trees are planted from 5 by 13 feet (1.5 by 4.0 m) apart in high-vigor sites to 4 by 12 feet (1.2 by 3.6 m) apart in low-vigor sites. Only highly self-fruitful, precocious varieties will fruit under the conditions of close spacing and heavy pruning. It also helps if the orchard manager can control soil water status to moderate tree vigor. It is anticipated that this system will be more difficult to manage in places with deep soils and high rainfall.

Sidebar 1.5
Two modern planting systems for olives

High-Density Hedgerow
- 8 × 16; 9 × 18; or 10 × 20 feet
- 2.4 × 4.9; 2.7 × 5.5; or 3.0 × 6.0 m
- 200 to 350 trees per acre (494 to 865 per ha)
- Bearing by the 5th year
- Full production by the 10th year
- Harvest by hand or shaker
- Highest cost is for harvest
- Low establishment cost

Super-High-Density
- 4 × 12 to 5 × 13 feet
- 1.2 × 3.6 to 1.5 × 4.0 m
- 600 to 900 trees per acre (1,482 to 2,223 per ha)
- Bearing by 3rd year
- Full production by 5th year
- Harvest: over-the-row
- Highest cost is pruning
- High establishment cost

PLANTING MATERIAL

Planting olive trees in the fall will get them settled into the soil and usually results in the best growth spurt in the spring, but beware of frost. Young container-grown trees are very susceptible to frost injury that first winter, so fall planting is more risky and should be done in areas with little danger of winter temperatures below 30°F (–1.1°C). To violate this rule puts young trees at risk of freezing, so most growers wait until the spring, in April and May, when the danger of frost is past. Olives are evergreen and are sold in 4-inch (10-cm) pots to 1-gallon (3.8-l) containers, not bare-root. The trees should be appropriately sized to the container so that the roots are not completely circling and root-bound. The ideal 1-gallon tree should be about 4 feet (1.2 m) tall with a single trunk and several lateral branches originating at about 30 to 36 inches (0.8 to 0.9 m). Trees in 4-inch pots are often cheaper but are smaller, about 18 inches (46 cm) tall, and will not grow quite as fast. Trees in 5-gallon (19-l) pots or larger produce a big tree more quickly, but they are more expensive and sometimes grow poorly if they have become root-bound in their containers.

Before planting, the trees should be well watered. Dig a hole about two times the diameter of the container, but not quite as deep. Remove the container and cut or spread any circling roots. Place the tree in the hole and place the surrounding soil back around the roots plus some additional soil from the surround-ing area so that the tree is planted slightly higher than the surrounding soil level. Make sure to cover the root ball with native soil. Don't mix large quantities of organic matter into the hole or backfill soil, because it can create an artificially good growing medium. If the backfill soil is a significantly better medium for root growth, the roots will continue to grow in it in a circle and never grow out into the native soil. After planting, place a thick layer of compost or mulch over the root zone to prevent weed growth and then water the trees in to settle the soil. If planted in the fall, the trees can be watered in with winter rains. If planted in the spring, the trees should have a drip emitter placed within a few inches of the root ball and should be watered lightly every day when the weather gets hot.

TREE TRAINING AND PRUNING

There are many different ways to prune olives, but a few general training forms predominate. The mini central leader is used in the super-high-density system to maintain a central trunk from which laterals are continuously renewed every 3 years, but that is a very intensive system and not the natural form in which olive trees grow. They normally grow in a basal form, which means that some lower laterals will grow just as vigorously as the leader. Consequently a bush is formed rather than a "Christmas tree" shape. The easiest way to manage this growth habit is to allow for the development of three to four main scaffold branches and by keeping the center open to maintain good light exposure in the lower portion of the tree.

In the high-density hedgerow system, the central leader tree form was believed to have some advantages for better fruit harvest, but that form is difficult to maintain and comes into bearing later. Recent research has also demonstrated that as the trees grow older, fruit removal with trunk shakers is very similar to removal with more easily managed tree forms such as the open center. The bush system attempts to keep the trees low for hand harvest, but hard pruning to limit tree size in olive trees often promotes excessively vigorous vegetative growth. The open-center-pruned olive tree is still the most popular.

Olive trees store most of their energy in their leaves, and unlike deciduous trees do not show much positive response to pruning. Pruning that removes significant amounts of foliage can stunt olives just like summer pruning, which removes leaves on deciduous trees. Consequently, olive growers do not prune their young trees very much or at all for the first 4 to 5 years. This has been demonstrated to allow trees to come into production 2 to 3 years earlier than if they were extensively trained at a young age. Once the trees are 10 feet (3 m) tall and are about 6 to 8 feet (1.8 to 2.4 m) wide, they should be opened up with some interior pruning. Removal of two to three interior upright branches with a small hand saw or large pruning loppers is sufficient. Repeating this for the next 3 to 4 years will open the center and allow for the selection of the permanent scaffold branches. Once the tree is about 8 years old and 12 to 15 feet (3.6 to 4.5 m) tall, it should have its permanent shape (plate 1.5).

Olive trees tend to be alternate bearing: heavy crops one year are usually followed by light crops the next year. Cultural practices such as hard pruning during flowering in heavy crop "on" years with excessive bloom should be employed to moderate crops from year to year. Many growers prune their olive trees every 2 years, in the year with an expected heavy crop load. Alternate bearing can also be reduced by providing adequate water and tree nutrition in years with a heavy crop load so that there is plenty of shoot growth for next year's crop (sidebar 1.6). Olive trees do not need to be staked; in fact, the strongest trees with the best root systems and trunks are not staked. Unstaked trees will usually be slightly shorter in stature. Unfortunately, staking is necessary in windy areas and for the super-high-density system to keep the young trees upright. In that system, trees can be individually staked with a fairly large, expensive stake or held upright with a cheaper small bamboo stake in combination with a single wire or twine attached to a large post placed about every 50 feet (15 m).

. . . .

REFERENCES

Barranco, D., R. Fernández-Escobar, and L. Rallo. 2001. El Cultivo del olivo. 4th ed. Madrid: Ediciones Mundi-Prensa.

Barranco, D., A. Cimato, P. Fiorino, L. Rallo, A. Touzani, C. Castañeda, F. Serafíni, and I. Trujillo. 2000. World catalogue of olive varieties. Madrid: International Olive Oil Council.

Berenguer, M. J., S. R. Grattan, J. H. Connell, V. S. Polito, and P. M. Vossen. 2003. Irrigation of olive trees. New AG International (Dec.). 64.

Berenguer, M. J., P. M. Vossen, S. R. Grattan, J. H. Connell, and V. S. Polito. 2006. Tree irrigation levels for optimum chemical and sensory properties of olive oil. HortScience 41(2): 427–432.

Cimato, A., A. Baldini, S. Caselli, M. Marronci, and L. Marzi. 1995. Observations on Tuscan olive germplasm. 3: Analytical and sensory characteristics of single-variety olive oils. Olivae Magazine 62:46–51.

Cimato, A., C. Cantini, G. Sani, and M. Marranci. 1997. Il Germoplasma dell' olivo in Toscana. Firenze: CNR.

Cirio, U. 1997. Agrochemicals and environmental impact in olive farming. Olivae Magazine 65:32–39.

Civantos López-Villalta, M. 1999. Olive pest and disease management. Madrid: International Olive Oil Council.

Goldhamer, D. A. 1999. Regulated deficit irrigation for California canning olives. Acta Horticulturae 47(1): 369–372.

Goldhamer, D. A., J. Dunai, and L. Ferguson. 1994. Irrigation requirements of olive trees and responses to sustained deficit irrigation. Acta Horticulturae 356:172–175.

Gonzálvez V., and R. Muñoz. 2002. La Olivicultura ecológica en España. Editora y Distribuidora El Olivo, S.L.L.

Grattan, S. R., M. J. Berenguer, J. H. Connell, V. S. Polito, and P. M. Vossen. 2006. Olive oil production as influenced by different quantities of applied water. Agricultural Water Mangagement 85:133–140.

Griggs, W. H., H. T. Hartman, M. V. Bradley, B. T. Iwakiri, and J. E. Whisler. 1975. Olive pollination in California. Berkeley: California Agricultural Experiment Station Bulletin 869.

Gucci, R., and C. Cantini. 2000. Pruning and training systems for modern olive growing. Victoria, Australia: CSIRO Publishing.

O'Malley, K., J. Bentivoglio, C. Beckingham, and D. Conlan. 2003. Organic olive management: A guide for Australian olive growers. Pendle Hill: New South Wales Agriculture and Australian Olive Association, www.australianolives.com.au.

Pastor, M., and J. Castro. 1995. Soil management systems and erosion. Olivae Magazine 59 (Dec.): 64–74.

Sibbett, G. S., and L. Ferguson, eds. 2005. Olive production manual. 2nd ed. Oakland: University of California Agriculture and Natural Resources Publication 3353.

Tous, J. M., A. Romero, and D. Barranco. 1993. Variedades del olivo. Barcelona: Ed. Fundaci n "La Caixa" – AEDOS.

Sidebar 1.6
Techniques to manage alternate bearing

On Year
- Prune more during bloom to reduce crop.
- Water more to increase shoot growth.
- Fertilize more to increase shoot growth.
- Good weed control to increase shoot growth.

Off Year
- Don't prune at all.
- Water less to reduce shoot growth and save water.
- Fertilize less to reduce shoot growth and save fertilizer.
- Some neglect is OK.

Tura, D., O. Failla, D. Bassi, and A. Serraiocco. 2000. Sensory and chemical analyses of monovarietal olive oils from Lake Garda (Northern Italy). In C. Vitagliano and G. P. Martelli, eds., Proceedings of 4th Intl. Symposium on Olive Growing. Acta Horticulturae 586:595–598.

Vossen, P. M. 2002a. Effective olive orchard management: Variety and maturity—The two largest influences on oil quality. Adelaide: Proceedings of the National Olive Industry Convention, Australian Olive Association. 60–63.

———. 2002b. Super-high-density olive oil production. OLINT Magazine Special English Edition 1 (Oct.).

———. 2003. Planting olive trees. Olea 6(2): 4–5.

———. 2004. Case study: Super-high-density olive oil production in California. Perth: Proceedings of the National Olive Industry Conference, Australian Olive Association.

———. 2005. Producing olive oil. In G. S. Sibbett and L. Ferguson, eds., Olive production manual. 2nd ed. Oakland: University of California Agriculture and Natural Resources Publication 3353. 157–173.

Vossen, P. M., L. Diggs, and L. Mendes. 2005. Sustainable agriculture education through crop diversity in commercial scale orchard crops (Establishment of a super-high-density organic olive oil orchard and a specialty organic apple orchard using recycled water at the SRJC Shone farm). Report to the California Food, Fiber, Future (CF-3) Program. Santa Rosa: University of California Cooperative Extension, Sonoma County.

2

Economics of Olive Oil Production

PAUL M. VOSSEN

OIL YIELDS

Oil yield per acre depends on several factors, primarily the amount of fruit per acre, the percentage of oil in the fruit, and the ability to extract it. Yields can range from less than 1 ton to 9 tons per acre (2 to 20 T/ha). A good consistent yield from year to year would be about 4 tons per acre (9 T/ha). Low yields are a function of poor shoot growth resulting from poor tree vigor caused by inadequate irrigation (dry-farmed), poor weed control, disease, very low fertility, inappropriate pruning, or a combination of these factors. It can also be caused by poor weather conditions during bloom, lack of chilling, frost damage, or inadequate flower pollination. Olives are strongly alternate bearing: a low crop yield one year will likely promote shoot growth, more flowers, and higher yields the following year. High yields are produced consistently only from orchards that are very well managed (table 2.1). Table 2.2 indicates the approximate theoretical quantity of oil produced from varying yields of olives per acre. The table shows the approximate oil yield from 1 ton of olives with different oil content and extractability.

Although the quantity of oil in the fruit is genetically determined, it can vary from year to year due to tree vigor, crop load, fruit maturity, and fruit moisture content. Oil content varies by variety from less than 10 percent to about 30 percent. Since oil accumulation peaks when the fruit is quite mature, delaying harvest until the fruit is ripe assures the highest yield of oil, although this will also change some flavor characteristics.

The fruit's water content influences the percentage of oil relative to moisture, so drier fruit will have a higher percentage of oil by weight. The extractability of the oil from the fruit is heavily influenced by fruit moisture content, maturity, and the extraction process; paste fineness, malaxation time and temperature, and extraction machinery type are the major factors. Some varieties give up their oil quite easily and others hold on to it as watery gels that escape with the fruit-water, or pomace, solids. Unripe, green fruit that has been overirrigated has high moisture content, and the oil is hard to extract. Ripe fruit with low moisture has a higher percentage of oil and the oil is easier to extract. It might be reasonable to expect a yield from oil varieties of about 3 to 4 tons per acre (6.7 to 9.0 T/ha) per year and to be able to extract about 40 gallons per ton (167 l/T) of oil from oil varieties, but there are so many variables that it is hard to be accurate with oil yield predictions. Table 2.2 indicates the approximate theoretical oil yield extracted from 1 ton of olives by variety, fruit moisture, and ripeness.

OIL OLIVE PRODUCTION COSTS

High-quality olive oil was once an exclusively Mediterranean product, but it is now produced in several other parts of the world, including California. The revival of the olive oil industry in California began in the North Coast coastal counties. There, land costs are extremely high and it is not likely that many large-scale olive oil producers will relocate in that area, though there is intense interest among small-scale producers and wineries in olive oil as an adjunct to their wine sales in tasting rooms. Widely spaced trees growing on scenic hillsides take many years to come into bearing and are expensive to produce. In order to make a profit, growers there must charge more for their oils. The Central Valley has cheaper, flatter land and less-expensive water and labor. Flat land makes for easier mechanical harvesting, which may be essential for competitive economic production of olive oil. The Central Valley and Sierra Nevada foothills have a great potential to produce both high-quality and high-volume olive oil at a much lower cost.

The two potential advantages for the North Coast counties is the association with fine wines for symbi-otic marketing relationships and the real or perceived difference in oil quality that is generally produced in cooler growing regions. It is likely, however, that the warmer Central Valley will have an agricultural advan-tage over the cooler coastal valleys when it comes to olive yields.

Table 2.1. Orchard conditions affecting fruit yields in oil olives

Fruit yield	Conditions affecting yield
1 ton per acre (2.24 T/ha)	• widely spaced orchard in the 5th to 6th year; or older orchard with close spacing that is shading out in the lower portions of the trees • poor irrigation, weed control, pruning, and nutrient management • excessively vigorous or weak growing conditions • poor pollination from rain, cold, drought stress, hot and dry wind during bloom, or inadequate pollinizer trees • alternate "off" year of production • super-high-density orchard in the 2nd year
2 tons per acre (4.48 T/ha)	• widely spaced orchard in the 6th to 8th year with excessive shading • poor irrigation, weed control, pruning, and nutrient management • excessively vigorous or weak growing conditions • poor pollination from rain, cold, drought stress, hot and dry wind during bloom, or inadequate pollinizer trees • alternate "off" year of production from very heavy production previous year • super-high-density orchard in the 3rd year
3 tons per acre (6.72 T/ha)	• properly spaced orchard in the 9th to 10th year with some shading • good irrigation, weed control, pruning, and nutrient management • acceptable vigor and growing conditions • some lack of pollination due to poor weather during bloom or a lack of pollinizer trees • probable maximum yield from a coastal hillside orchard • super-high-density orchard in the 3rd year
4 tons per acre (8.96 T/ha)	• properly spaced orchard in the 10th+ year with little or no shading • very good irrigation, weed control, pruning, and nutrient management • correct vigor and growing conditions • very good pollination and weather conditions • sustainable yield under very good management • well-managed super-high-density orchard in the 4th+ year
5 tons per acre (11.2 T/ha)	• properly spaced orchard in the 10th+ year with no shading • excellent irrigation, weed control, pruning, and nutrient management • ideal vigor and growing conditions • excellent pollination and weather conditions • alternate "on" year of production from a low yield previous year • very well-managed super-high-density orchard in the 4th+ year
> 6 tons per acre* (> 13.44 T/ha)	• properly spaced orchard in the 10th+ year with no shading • superior irrigation, weed control, pruning, and nutrient management • ideal vigor and growing conditions • ideal pollination and weather conditions • unsustainable yield from alternate "on" year of production from a very low yield previous year • superior management in a super-high-density orchard in the 4th+ year

Note: * Yields have been recorded in table olives in California at 12 tons per acre (26.9 T/ha). This is usually preceded by a light crop and followed by a very light crop.

Table 2.2. Approximate oil yield from 1 ton (0.907 T) of olives with various oil content and extractability

Variety	Ripeness	Water status	Oil yield gal/ton (l/T)	Oil % on net weight basis
Sevillano	green	overwatered	10 (41.7)	4%
Sevillano	ripe	well-watered	15 (62.6)	6%
Ascolano	green	overwatered		
Sevillano	very ripe	deficit-irrigated	20 (83.5)	8%
Ascolano	ripe	well-watered		
Arbequina or Manzanillo	green	overwatered	25 (104.3)	9.5%
Ascolano	very ripe	deficit-irrigated		
Arbequina or Manzanillo	ripe	overwatered	30 (125.2)	11%
Frantoio or Leccino	green	overwatered		
Arbequina or Manzanillo	very ripe	well-watered	35 (146.1)	13%
Mission	green	overwatered		
Frantoio or Leccino	ripe	overwatered		
Frantoio or Leccino	ripe	well-watered	40 (166.9)	15%
Mission	green	well-watered		
Arbequina or Manzanillo		deficit-irrigated		
Mission	ripe	overwatered	45 (187.8)	17%
Frantoio or Leccino	ripe	deficit-irrigated		
Mission or Picual	ripe	well-watered	50 (208.7)	19%
Mission or Picual	very ripe	deficit-irrigated	55 (229.5)	21%

High-Density Coastal Orchard Production Costs

In 1999 and 2001, University of California cost studies were completed on the establishment of an olive orchard and production costs for olive oil on the North Coast and Central Coast of California (Vossen et al. 1999, 2001). Production costs in these two studies were based on typical coastal orchards with high cultural costs and mediocre yields.

According to these studies, first-year establishment costs were about $4,500 per acre ($11,115 per ha). For a mature producing orchard, which takes 8 to 10 years to come into full production, an average yield of 2.5 tons per acre (5.6 T/ha) was used. The following approximate costs per acre were calculated as an example:

$1,000	Cultural operations (pest control, pruning, irrigation, mowing, etc.)
$ 900	Harvest and transport (hand-harvest at $360/ton)
$ 900	Processing (custom-milling and separation at $360/ton)
$2,000	Oil transport, storage, bottling, and labeling
$1,500	Marketing
$ 500	Overhead (office, taxes, insurance, etc.)
$2,200	Capital recovery (land, buildings, & investment)

$9,000	Total approximate cost per acre
$3,600	Total approximate cost per ton
$ 80	Total approximate cost per gallon

With a yield of 2.5 tons per acre and an oil yield of 45 gallons per ton, 112.5 gallons of oil are produced per acre, or 852 500-ml bottles (71 cases), at a cost of $9,000—over $10.50 per bottle. Retailers add from 40 to 100 percent mark up for upper-end, low-volume products, so the oil would have to sell for about $20.00 per bottle at retail stores just to meet costs. Clearly, in order to make a profit, either the price per bottle or yield per acre would have to be higher, or the production costs would have to be much lower. The volume of oil sold at such high prices is quite limited, especially when equivalent or nearly equivalent oil can be obtained for a much lower cost.

Super-High-Density Central Valley Production Costs

Several scenarios are being pursued in the olive oil industry in an attempt to lower production costs and get the wholesale price of a 500-ml bottle down to around $5.00. Efforts are also being made to raise annual production yields to around 5 tons per acre (11.2 T/ha), which is entirely possible.

Most retailers feel that a retail price of $10.00 per bottle would be competitive and lead to a fairly high sales volume. One way to reach this price is to eliminate the intermediary and much of the marketing cost by selling directly to the consumer through mail order, the Internet, farmers' markets, or winery tasting room sales. Another is to place the overhead and land-related costs onto some other part of the operation, ignore them completely, or at least grow olives on lower-cost land.

Another approach is to reduce production costs, which mostly means reducing labor. The super-high-density system makes sense in its attempt to reduce production costs by reducing labor for harvest and other cultural practices. Though initial investment is high, the varieties grown come into bearing early, which improves the speed of return on investment; the low stature of the trees makes them more efficient to prune and spray; and the continuous-flow straddle harvester (almost like a combine harvesting grain) can harvest almost 2 acres (1 ha) per hour with only two workers (plate 2.1).

In 2004, a group of UC researchers produced another cost study for establishing and producing a super-high-density olive orchard in the Sacramento Valley of California (Vossen et al. 2004). This cost study used specific varieties that could be produced in the super-high-density system, harvested mechanically with an over-the-row modified grape harvester, and grown with all the cultural costs associated with labor rates and so on in that production area. The trees come into bearing earlier: full production occurs in the fourth year, with significant yield in the third year, plus some harvestable fruit in the second year. This is comparable to wine grapes, for example. Total annual yields will be about 5 tons per acre thereafter. First-year establishment costs were $5,420 per acre. The following approximate production costs, per acre, were calculated as an example:

$ 700   Cultural operations (pest control, pruning, irrigation, mowing, etc.)
$ 200   Harvest and transport (mechanical at $40/ton)
$1,000   Processing (custom-milling and separation at $200/ton)
$3,500   Oil transport, storage, bottling, and labeling
$1,500   Marketing
$ 400   Overhead (office, taxes, insurance, etc.)
$1,100   Capital recovery (land, buildings, & investment)

$8,400   Total approximate cost per acre
$1,680   Total approximate cost per ton
$ 38   Total approximate cost per gallon

With a yield of 5 tons per acre and an oil yield of 45 gallons per ton, 225 gallons of oil are produced per acre, or 1,704 500-ml bottles (142 cases), at a cost of $8,400—$4.93 per bottle. The potential retail price would be around $10.00. The mechanized Central Valley orchard is producing olive oil for half the cost of the North Coast or Central Coast orchard in the previous example.

....

ECONOMIC COMPARISON OF CALIFORNIA COASTAL WINE AND OLIVE OIL

Since wine grape plantings have been so common over the last few years and somewhat profitable in the coastal and foothill areas of California, it is advisable (at least theoretically) to compare the costs and returns between wine and olive oil production. It is also interesting to see the differences between the costs and returns of the raw product sold to a processor (sidebar 2.1). Wine grape yields per acre are the same to about double that of olives. Olives produce about 2 to 3 tons per acre (4.5 to 6.7 T/ha) (a range of 1 to 5), and wine grapes produce about 5 tons per acre (11.2 T/ha) (a range of 2 to 8). Wine grapes also produce about four times more volume of liquid per acre than do olives, 45 gallons of oil per ton (188 l/ha) of olives versus about 170 gallons of wine per ton (709 l/ha) of grapes.

Coastal hillside red wine cultural costs are $3,000 per acre ($7,400/ha), which is $2,000 higher than the cultural costs for oil olives grown under similar conditions at a tree spacing of 11 by 22 feet (3.4 by 6.7 m) (sidebar 2.2). The higher cost for wine grape production is due to the need for more extensive pruning, pest control, and plant manipulations. Costs to harvest and process grapes into wine are similar to olive oil, about $2,000 per acre ($4,900/ha). The bottling and labeling costs are $1,600 higher, because there are many more bottles produced, 3,600 750-ml bottles of wine compared with 852 500-ml bottles of olive oil. The overhead and capital recovery costs are similar except that the wine grape land values are higher, making land payments higher by about $400 per acre ($990/ha). The ultimate cost to produce a bottle of red

Sidebar 2.1
Economic comparison of oil olives and wine grape production

Oil Olives

Coastal hillside, specialty varieties

$1,000	cultural cost
$ 900	hand-harvest at $360/ton
$ 500	overhead (office, taxes, insurance)
$2,200	capital recovery (land, buildings, equipment)
$4,600	total cost per acre

- Cost of yield at 2.5 tons per acre = $1,840/ton
- Establishment cost = $11,128 (3 yr).
- 10 years to come into production

Wine Grapes

Coastal hillside, red

$3,000	cultural cost
$ 500	hand-harvest
$1,500	overhead (office, taxes, insurance)
$2,600	capital recovery (land, buildings, equipment)
$7,000	total cost per acre

- Cost of yield at 5 tons per acre = $1,400/ton
- Establishment cost = $23,709 (3 yr)
- 5 years to come into full production

Sidebar 2.2
Economic comparison of olive oil and wine production

Olive Oil

Coastal hillside

$1,000	cultural cost
$ 900	hand harvest at $360/ton
$ 900	processing cost at $360/ton
$2,000	bottling, labeling, storage
$1,500	marketing and promotion
$ 500	overhead (office, taxes, insurance)
$2,200	capital recovery (land, buildings, equipment)
$9,000	total cost per acre ($3,600/ton)

- Yield of 2.5 tons per acre = 852 bottles (500 ml)
- Cost per bottle = $11.20
- 10 years to come into production

Red Wine

Coastal hillside

$3,000	cultural cost
$2,000	harvesting, crushing, and fermenting
$3,600	bottling, labeling, and storage
$5,000	marketing and promotion
$1,500	overhead (office, taxes, insurance)
$2,600	capital recovery (land, buildings, equipment)
$18,200	total cost per acre ($3,640/ton)

- Yield of 5 tons per acre = 3,600 bottles (750 ml)
- Cost per bottle = $5.05
- 5 years to come into full production

coastal hillside wine is around $5.00 per bottle, which is less than half the cost to produce olive oil. Wine grapes also come into full production in half the time, so the return on investment is faster.

The first 3 years of establishment costs for an acre of olives on the North Coast of California is about half of what it takes to put in wine grapes and get them into production: $11,128 for olives and $23,700 for wine grapes. This is because the permit requirements for wine grapes are higher, and wine grapes, in these specific studies, required more plants per acre, an extensive trellis system, intricate training, and an overhead sprinkler frost protection system.

The cost per acre to produce wine grapes is almost double that of oil olives, $7,000 for wine grapes compared with $4,000 for oil olives, but the yield for wine grapes is higher, so the costs per ton are fairly similar, with the olives costing $440 more per ton ($400/T) to produce. If the processing part is removed so that the grower sells either the wine grapes or olives in bulk to a processor, the break-even price would be $1,840 per ton ($1,668/T) for olives and $1,400 per ton ($1,270/T) for the wine grapes.

In 2003, raw olive fruit was commonly sold for $300 to $500 per ton ($272 to $454/T) from semiabandoned orchards in the Sacramento Valley foothills. Small quantities of specialty oil varieties (Tuscan Blend) were sold for about $1,000 per ton ($907/T). Specialty olive oil varieties are not usually sold as bulk raw olives since most growers are producing and marketing their own oil. Approximate wine grape prices for North Coast red varieties were about $2,000 per ton ($1,818/T) to the grower in 2003, based on the CDFA grape crush report (NASS 2004).

....

THE MARKET FOR OLIVE OIL

The United States imports over 60 million gallons (5,600,000 hl) of olive oil annually, and consumers buy about three-quarters of a liter per person per year. California's production of 400,000 gallons per year, grown on about 8,000 acres (3238 ha), is only 0.6 percent of what is consumed in the United States.

California producers would have to plant over 300,000 acres (121,410 ha) of olives to offset what is currently imported. If the demand for olive oil continues to increase at a rate of about 10 percent per year, as it has for the last ten years, then even more acres would have to be planted to meet domestic demand. The current planting rate is about 2,000 acres (809 ha) per year.

CONCLUSION

With mechanization and lower land costs in the Central Valley it appears that olive oil can be produced at a much lower cost there than in the coastal areas. Using cost and production data from olive oil production in the Sacramento Valley and the mechanized super-high-density system, compared with cost and production data for wine grapes on the North Coast, we can see that wine grapes should be grown on the coast and olives should be grown in the Valley. Coastal olive oil producers will have to find a way to add value to their product just like they have for every other agricultural commodity, through local direct sales, raising the price based on quality associated with the growing region, developing more esoteric styles of oil, or some other specialty niche.

Based on taste tests conducted by the University of California Taste Panel, California olive oils appear to be able to compete qualitatively with imported European oils. Many California olive oils have also received numerous awards in international competitions and in domestic competitions against imported olive oils. In a few cases California olive oils have won "Best of Show" in blind international competitions. One example is the Lunigiana brand olive oil produced in Glen Ellen, California, which won the 2002 Ecoliva competition for best organic olive oil in the world. Another is the 2006 Los Angeles Fair Best of Show award for domestic olive oil won by California Olive Ranch, which was produced in Oroville, California. Another example is DaVero olive oil. DaVero was the first American olive oil to win a blind tasting in Italy (Imperia, 1997), was chosen as the Top Tuscan Oil of the Year (Gambero Rosso, 1998), and received the gold medal at the Olive Oils of the World Competition in both 2002 and 2003.

The huge domestic market for olive oil is not being met by domestic supply. Most people in the industry feel that if California can continue to produce excellent olive oil at a competitive price, the market is for the taking. They cite the positive examples of the wine and almond industries in which California producers have been able to compete favorably with Europe in quality, price, or both.

REFERENCES

NASS (USDA National Agricultural Statistics Service). 2004. Grape crush report. NASS Web site, http://www.nass.usda.gov/ca/bul/crush/indexgcb.htm.

Senise Barrio, O., and H. Carman. 2005. Olive oil a "rediscovered" California crop. University of California Giannini Foundation Update (May/June) 8(5): 1–4. University of California, Davis, Department of Agricultural and Resource Economics Web site, http://www.agecon.ucdavis.edu/uploads/update_articles/v8n5_1.pdf.

Smith, R. J., K. Klonsky, P. Livingston, and R. L. De Moura. 2004. Sample costs to establish a vineyard and produce wine grapes, Chardonnay, North Coast Region, Sonoma County. University of California, Davis, Department of Agricultural and Resource Economics Web site, http://www.coststudies.ucdavis.edu/uploads/cost_return_articles/grapewinenc2004.pdf.

Vossen, P. M. 2001. Producing olive oil. In G. S. Sibbett and L. Ferguson, eds., Olive production manual. 2nd ed. Oakland: University of California Agriculture and Natural Resources Publication 3353. 157–173.

———. 2006. Olive oil yield: Factors affecting production. First Press Newsletter 2(1): 1–2. http://ucce.ucdavis.edu/files/filelibrary/2161/29131.pdf

Vossen, P. M., and A. Devarenne. 2005. California olive oil industry survey statistics: 2004. UC Cooperative Extension Sonoma County Web site, http://cesonoma.ucdavis.edu/hortic/pdf/olive_oil_survey_05.pdf.

Vossen, P. M., G. S. Sibbett, R. Evers, K. Klonsky, and P. Livingston. 1999. Sample costs to establish an olive orchard and produce olive oil, North Coast of California. University of California, Davis, Department of Agricultural and Resource Economics Web site, http://coststudies.ucdavis.edu/uploads/cost_return_articles/99oliveoil.pdf.

Vossen, P. M., K. Klonsky, and R. L. De Moura. 2001. Sample costs to establish an olive orchard and produce olive oil, Central Coast of California. University of California, Davis, Department of Agricultural and Resource Economics Web site, http://coststudies.ucdavis.edu/uploads/cost_return_articles/2001oliveoil.pdf.

Vossen, P. M., J. H. Connell, K. Klonsky, and P. Livingston. 2004. Sample costs to establish a super-high-density olive orchard and produce oil, Sacramento Valley. University of California, Davis, Department of Agricultural and Resource Economics Web site, http://coststudies.ucdavis.edu/uploads/cost_return_articles/oliveoilsv2004.pdf.

Weber, E., K. Klonsky, and R. L. De Moura. 2003. Sample costs to establish a vineyard and produce wine grapes, Cabernet Sauvignon, North Coast region, Napa County. University of California, Davis, Department of Agricultural and Resource Economics Web site, http://coststudies.ucdavis.edu/uploads/cost_return_articles/grapewinenapa03.pdf.

3

International Olive Oil Council Trade Standard for Olive Oil

PAUL M. VOSSEN

DEFINITION OF GRADES

The International Olive Oil Council (IOOC) has a United Nations charter to develop criteria standards for olive oil quality and purity. Their main focus is regulating the legal aspects of the olive oil industry and preventing unfair competition. The standards they have developed are recognized by the vast majority of the world's olive oil producers and marketers. The international standards under resolution COI/T.15/NC no 3-25 (revised June 2003) lists nine grades of olive oil under two primary categories: olive oil and olive pomace oil. This section presents the official definitions from section 2 of the standards for each of the nine grades.

The IOOC standard oils must meet certain criteria for inclusion into specific categories. The olive oils must not be adulterated with any other type of oil, must pass a sensory analysis by a certified panel of tasters, and must meet the analytical criteria. The standard indicates all the tests used to determine genuineness and purity along with the legal requirements for the label. Olive oil is defined as oil obtained solely from fruit of the olive tree (*Olea europaea* L.). Virgin oils are obtained solely by mechanical means that do not lead to alterations in the oil (table 3.1).

§ 2.1 Olive Oil Category

Oil obtained solely from the fruit of the olive tree (*Olea europa* L.) to the exclusion of oils obtained using solvents or re-esterification processes and of any mixture with other kinds of oils (seed or nut oils).

2.1.1 Virgin Olive Oils: Obtained solely by mechanical or physical means under thermal conditions that do not lead to alterations in the oil; using only treatments such as washing, decantation, centrifugation, and filtration.

2.1.1.1 Those fit for human consumption are as follows:

- **Extra Virgin Olive Oil:** This oil, as evaluated numerically by the mean of a certified taste panel, contains zero (0) defects and greater than zero positive attributes. In other words, more than half of the tasters indicated that it is not defective and has some fruitiness. Extra virgin oil also must have a free acidity percentage of less than 0.8 and conform to all the standards listed in its category. This is the highest quality rating for an olive oil. Extra virgin olive oil should have clear flavor characteristics that reflect the fruit from which it was made. In relation to the complex matrix of variety, fruit maturity, growing region, and extraction technique, good olive oils can be very different from one another, but can all be classified as extra virgin.

- **Virgin Olive Oil:** This is oil with a sensory analysis rating of the mean of tasters, having defects from 0 to less than 2.5, a free acidity of less than 2 percent, and conforms to all the other standards in its category. These are oils with analytical and sensory indices that reflect slightly lower quality than extra virgin olive oil.

- **Ordinary Virgin Olive Oil:** Oil with a lower organoleptic rating (defects from the mean of tasters 2.5 to less than 6.0), a free acidity of less than 3.3 percent, and conformity within its category for all other standards. This is inferior oil with notable defects and is not permitted to be bottled under European Union (EU) laws, so it is sent for refining. The EU has eliminated this category and other regulating agencies are likely to follow. It will simply be absorbed into the lampante category.

Table 3.1. Purity standards for olive oil

Sterol content (olive oil and pomace oil)	(%)
cholesterol	max 0.5
brassicasterol	max 0.1
campesterol	max 4.0
stigmasterol	< campesterol
D-7 stigmastenol	max 0.5
beta-sitosterol + D-5 avenasterol + D 5-23 stigmastadienol + cleroesterol+ sitostanol + D-524 stigmastadienol	min 93

Total sterols	(mg/kg)
virgin, refined and olive oil	min 1,000
crude pomace oil	min 2,500
refined olive oil	min 1,800
pomace oil	min 1,600

Fatty acid composition (olive oil)	(% mm of methyl esters)
myristic acid c 14:0	max 0.05
palmitic acid c 16:0	7.5–20.0
palmitoleic acid c 16:1	0.3–3.5
heptadecanoic acid c 17:0	max 0.3
heptadecenoic acid c 17:1	max 0.3
stearic acid c 18:0	0.5–5.0
oleic acid c 18:1	55.0–83.0
linoleic acid c 18:2	3.5–21.0
linolenic acid c 18:3	max 1.0 (EU: 0.9)
arachidic acid c 20:0	max 0.6
gadoleic acid c 20:1	max 0.4
behenic acid c 22:0	max 0.2 (pomace oils: max 0.3)
lignoceric c 24:0	max 0.2

Saturated fatty acids in 2 position	(%)
virgin olive oil	max 1.5 (EU: 1.3)
refined olive oil	max 1.8 (EU: 1.5)
olive oil	max 1.8 (EU: 1.5)
crude pomace oil	max 2.2 (EU: 2.0)
refined pomace oil	max 2.2 (EU: 2.0)

Unsaponifiable material	(g/kg)
olive oil	max 15
pomace oil	max 30

Pomace oil detection	Waxes (mg/kg)	Erythrodiol + uvaol (%)
virgin olive oil	max 250	max 4.5
lamp virgin olive oil	max 350 (EU: 300)	max 4.5
refined olive oil	max 350	max 4.5
olive oil	max 350	max 4.5

Seed oil detection (maximum difference between real and theoretical ECN 42 content)	(%)
virgin olive oil	0.2
lamp virgin olive oil	0.3
refined olive oil	0.3
olive oil	0.3
pomace oil	0.5

Refined vegetable oil detection	Stigmastadienes (ppm)	R1 (ppm)
virgin olive oil	max 0.15	—
lamp virgin olive oil	max 0.50	—
refined olive oil	max 50.0	min 12.0
olive oil	max 50.0	min 12.0
crude pomace oil	max 5.0	no limit
refined pomace oil	max 120.0	min 10
pomace oil	max 120.0	min 10

Trans fatty acid content	C:181 T (%)	C 18:2 T + C 18:3 T (%)
virgin olive oil	< 0.05	< 0.05
lamp virgin olive oil	max 0.10	max 0.10
refined olive oil	max 0.20	max 0.30
olive oil	max 0.20	max 0.30
crude pomace oil	max 0.20	max 0.10
refined pomace oil	max 0.40	max 0.35
pomace oil	max 0.40	max 0.35

Source: IOOC 2003.

2.1.1.2 Virgin Olive Oil Not Fit for Human Consumption (Lampante): Oil with severe defects (greater than 6.0) or free acidity of greater than 3.3 percent, and which conforms to the other standards within its category. It is not fit for human consumption because of flavor defects and must be refined. These oils come from bad fruit or from improper handling and processing.

2.1.2 Refined Olive Oil Not Fit for Human Consumption: Oil obtained from virgin oils by refining methods that do not alter the initial glyceride structure. It has a free acidity of less than 0.3 and must conform to the other standards within its category. The origin of refined olive oil must not come from the solvent extraction of pomace. The refining process usually consists of treating virgin oil/lampante with sodium hydroxide to neutralize the free acidity, washing, drying, odor removal, color removal, and filtration. In the process, the oil can be heated to as high as 430°F (220°C) under a vacuum to remove all of the volatile components. Refined olive oil is usually odorless, tasteless, and colorless. It is not fit for human consumption in many countries including the EU due to poor flavor, not because of a safety concern.

2.1.3 Olive Oil: Oils that are a blend of refined and unrefined virgin oils. It must have a free acidity of not more than 1 percent and conform to the other standards within its category. This grade of oil actually represents the bulk of the oil sold on the world market to the consumer. Blends are made in proportions to create specific styles and prices. Oils in the United States labeled as "Extra Light" would most likely be a blend dominated by refined olive oil. Other blends with more color and flavor would contain more virgin or extra virgin olive oil.

§ 2.2 Olive Pomace Oil

Oil obtained by treating olive pomace with solvents. It does not include oils obtained in the re-esterification processes or any mixture with oils of other kinds (seed or nut oils).

2.2.1 Crude Olive-Pomace Oil Not Fit for Human Consumption: This is the solvent-extracted crude oil product as it comes out of the pomace extractor after distillation to separate and recover most of the solvent. EU law also defines any oil containing 300 to 350 mg/kg of waxes and aliphatic alcohols above 350 mg/kg to be crude pomace oil. It is not fit for human consumption because it contains solvents and must be refined.

2.2.2 Refined Olive-Pomace Oil Not Fit for Human Consumption: Oil obtained from crude pomace oil by refining methods that do not alter the initial glyceride structure. It has a free acidity of not more than 0.3 percent and its other characteristics must conform to the standard in its category. Refining includes the same methods used for "refined olive oil" except that the source of the raw product comes from pomace by means of solvent extraction. It is not fit for human consumption in many countries and under EU laws, due to flavor considerations.

2.2.3 Olive-Pomace Oil: A blend of refined olive-pomace oil and virgin olive oil that is fit for human consumption. It has a free acidity of not more than 1 percent and must conform to the other standards within its category. In no case shall this blend be called "olive oil" (plate 3.1).

. . . .

SENSORY CHARACTERISTICS

One of the most important aspects of olive oil classification and value determination is sensory analysis. Human sensory evaluation through taste is much more accurate (100 times) for olive oil than laboratory equipment for certain characteristics. Aroma and taste are very complex and cannot be determined in the laboratory. The tongue can also detect texture differences difficult to measure analytically. The first and primary objective in sensory evaluation of olive oil is to determine whether the oil contains one or more of the defects that commonly occur in oils from improper fruit storage, handling, pest infestation, oil storage, or processing problems. Olive oil should have

a fresh fruity olive flavor that is characteristic of the variety or blend of varieties making up the oil. There should be no vinegary or fermented odor or flavor. The oil should also not be rancid or possess any other off flavor that is essentially not of the olive. The second objective of sensory evaluation of oil is to describe the positive characteristics of the oil relative to its intensity of olive-fruity character. Bitterness and pungency are often present in olive oils, especially when newly made. They are not defects and will mellow as the oils age.

The numerical sensory values for each of the first three grades (extra virgin, virgin, and ordinary virgin) come from a rating of the oil by a qualified taste panel that has been officially recognized by the IOOC. The majority of the tasters—usually 5 of 8—must agree statistically on the rating of the oil indicating the same defect, if any is present, and similar intensity for fruitiness, bitterness, and pungency.

The University of California and the California Olive Oil Council (COOC) have established a recognized sensory evaluation taste panel using the methods outlined by the IOOC. The University of California Research Panel meets periodically to evaluate olive oils from UC research and educational projects. The COOC portion of the panel meets to certify oils for its members. The University of California has served to ensure an unbiased analysis of oils and suitable training of official tasters (plate 3.2).

Standards are promulgated by the International Organization for Standardization (ISO), http://www.iso.com; American Oil Chemists Society (AOCS), http://www.aocs.org; and the International Union of Pure and Applied Chemistry (IUPAC) http://www.iupac.org.

Guidelines for Tasting Olive Oil

- Taste oil in mid-morning.

- Don't eat anything or have any foreign flavors in your mouth before tasting (no smoking, toothpaste, gum, candy, lipstick, coffee, etc.).

- Don't have foreign smells on your hands or body such as perfumes or aftershave.

- Find a room that is quiet and free of any odor.

- Sit down, relax, and take your time (5 to 15 minutes per oil).

- Taste about 4 to 5 oils and no more than 10 oils at any one time.

- Rinse your palate with sour apple (Granny Smith variety) and water between oils.

- Use some sort of recording sheet that identifies date, oil sample, name, and attributes.

- If possible remove the bias of color from your tasting by using a colored glass.

- Swirl the glass with a cover on it or use your hand to cover the glass.

- Warm the oil to about body temperature before smelling or tasting it. It should not be cold or hot as you put it into your mouth.

- Remove the cover or your hand and immediately smell the oil by taking a big whiff.

- Drink about 3 to 5 ml (1/2 to 1 tsp) of the oil, but before swallowing it, suck in air and swirl it around your entire mouth for about 10 seconds. Swallow it, close your mouth and breathe out through your nose.

- Immediately write down your impressions: first impressions are usually the best.

Positive Attributes (Defined by the IOOC)

- **Fruity:** Set of the olfactory sensations characteristic of the oil, which depends on the variety and comes from sound, fresh olives, either ripe or unripe. It is perceived directly or through the back of the nose (retronasal).

- **Bitter:** Characteristic taste of oil obtained from unripe olives. Perceived on the back of the tongue.

- **Pungent:** "Picante," or biting, tactile sensation characteristic of certain olive varieties or oil produced from unripe olives. Perceived in the throat.

Negative Attributes (Defined by the IOOC)

- **Fusty:** Characteristic flavor of oil obtained from olives stored in piles, which have undergone an advanced stage of anaerobic fermentation (plate 3.3). Associated with n-octane, produced from the decomposition of 10-hydroperoxide of oleic acid and isoamyl alcohol formed from fermentation.

- **Musty:** Characteristic moldy flavor of oils obtained from fruit in which large numbers of fungi and yeast have developed as a result of the oil being stored in humid conditions for several days.

- **Muddy sediment:** Characteristic flavor of oil that has been left in contact with the sediment in tanks and vats.

- **Winey-vinegary:** Characteristic flavor of certain oils reminiscent of wine or vinegar. This flavor is mainly due to aerobic fermentation in the olives, leading to the formation of acetic acid, ethyl acetate, and ethanol.

- **Rancid:** Flavor of oils that have undergone a process of oxidation and a fragmentation of hydroperoxides into compounds with characteristic disagreeable odors such as aldehydes, ketones, acids, alcohols, lactones, furans, and esters.

- **Heated or burnt:** Characteristic flavor of oils caused by excessive and/or prolonged heating during processing.

- **Hay or woody:** Characteristic flavor of certain oil produced from olives that have dried out or were frozen.

- **Greasy:** Flavor of oil reminiscent of that of diesel oil, grease, or mineral oil.

- **Vegetable water:** Flavor acquired by the oil as a result of prolonged contact with the liquid, nonoil fraction of the olive, also called fruit-water.

- **Brine:** Flavor of oil extracted from olives that have been preserved in brine.

- **Earthy:** Flavor of oil obtained from olives that have been collected with earth or mud on them and not washed.

OTHER IOOC STANDARDS

- **Color:** A subjective visual rating made of an oil to make sure it does not have unusual color that is not common to olive oil. Color can also be evaluated using a spectrophotometer according to the International Union of Pure Applied Chemistry (IUPAC) methods for specific hue, purity, and brightness (table 3.2).

- **Aspect:** A subjective visual rating made to determine whether the oil is clear (limpid) or cloudy

Table 3.2. Olive oil criteria and standards, 2003

	Extra virgin	Virgin	Ordinary virgin	Lamp* virgin	Refined olive	Olive oil	Crude pomace	Refined pomace	Olive pomace
Sensory characteristics									
median of defects	= 0	0 ≤ 2.5	2.5 < 6.0†	> 6.0	accept-able	good	—	accept-able	good
median of fruitiness	> 0	> 0	—	—	—	—	—	—	—
Color	—	—	—	—	yellow	yellow to green	—	light to dark yellow	yellow to green
Aspect	—	—	—	—	limpid	limpid	—	limpid	limpid
Free acidity percent	≤ 0.8	≤ 2.0	≤ 3.3	≤ 3.3	≤ 0.3	≤ 1.5	no limit	≤ 0.3	≤ 1.5
Peroxide value (meq O_2/kg)	≤ 20	≤ 20	≤ 20	no limit	≤ 5	≤ 15	no limit	≤ 5	≤ 15
UV absorbency									
232 nm*	≤ 2.5	≤ 2.6	—	—	—	—	—	—	—
270 nm	≤ 0.22	≤ 0.25	≤ 0.30‡	—	≤ 1.10	≤ 0.90	—	≤ 2.00	≤ 1.70
K	≤ 0.01	≤ 0.01	≤ 0.01	—	≤ 0.16	≤ 0.15	—	≤ 0.20	≤ 0.18
H_2O and volatiles (%)	≤ 0.2	≤ 0.2	≤ 0.2	≤ 0.3	≤ 0.1	≤ 0.1	≤ 1.5	≤ 0.1	≤ 0.1
Insoluble impurities (%)	≤ 0.1	≤ 0.1	≤ 0.1	≤ 0.2	≤ 0.05	≤ 0.05	—	≤ 0.05	≤ 0.05
Flash point (°C)	—	—	—	—	—	—	> 120°C	—	—
Metal traces (mg/kg)									
iron	≤ 3.0	≤ 3.0	≤ 3.0	≤ 3.0	≤ 3.0	≤ 3.0	—	≤ 3.0	≤ 3.0
copper	≤ 0.1	≤ 0.1	≤ 0.1	≤ 0.1	≤ 0.1	≤ 0.1	—	≤ 0.1	≤ 0.1
Halogenated solvents (mg/kg)									
each solvent	≤ 0.1	≤ 0.1	≤ 0.1	—	≤ 0.1	≤ 0.1	—	≤ 0.1	≤ 0.1
sum of solvents	≤ 0.2	≤ 0.2	≤ 0.2	—	≤ 0.2	≤ 0.2	—	≤ 0.2	≤ 0.2

Source: IOOC 2003.

Notes:

* It is not obligatory for the criteria of organoleptic characteristics, acidity, peroxide value, or absorbency to be concurrent; one is sufficient.

† Or, when the median defect is lower than or equal to 2.5 and the fruity median is 0.

‡ After passage of the sample through activated aluminum, absorbency at 270 nm shall be equal to or less than 0.11.

after it has been maintained at a temperature of 68°F (20°C) for 24 hours. Aspect can indicate the abnormal presence of saturated fatty acids in olive oil.

- **Free acidity:** A crude indicator of the quality of the fruit and handling procedures prior to milling. It is a measurement of hydrolytic breakdown of the fatty acid chains from triglycerides into diglycerides and monoglycerides, liberating free fatty acids. It is determined easily with a titration of potassium hydroxide that neutralizes the acidity. Free acidity is usually expressed as the percentage of free fatty acids on the basis of the oleic acid, because that

is the predominant fatty acid in olive oil, and is commonly called the percent acidity or free acidity percent. Free acidity in an oil is not the same as sourness or acidity in other foods. Free fatty acids (acidity) cannot be tasted in olive oil, at least not at the levels normally present.

- **Peroxide value:** A crude indicator of the amount of primary oxidation that has occurred, forming peroxide compounds in the oil. A high value indicates that the olives or paste were likely handled improperly and that the oil could be defective and might not keep well. The determination is made by a titration that liberates iodine from potassium iodide and is expressed as a value in milliequivalents of free oxygen per kilogram of oil (meq O_2/kg).

- **UV light absorbency:** A more delicate indicator of oxidation, especially in oils that have been heated in the refining process. It measures the quantity of certain oxidized compounds that resonate at wavelengths of 232 and 270 nanometers (nm) in the ultraviolet spectrum in a spectrophotometer. Delta (Δ) K detects whether oil has been treated with color-removing substances and also indicates the presence of refined or pomace oil by measuring the difference between absorbance at 270 nm and 266 nm to 274 nm.

- **Moisture and volatiles:** A measure of the water and volatile material content that may be present by placing a measured weight of oil in a drying stove for 30 minutes for a series of periods and measuring the weight difference until a difference is no longer detected. It is expressed as a percentage of the total weight.

- **Insoluble impurities:** A measure of the presence of dirt, minerals, resins, oxidized fatty acids, alkaline soaps of palmitic and stearic acids, and proteins that are suspended in the oil. It is determined by dissolving a quantity of oil in petroleum ether and filtering out the impurities and is expressed as a percentage of the total.

- **Flash point:** A measure of the temperature at which the sample spontaneously begins to burn. Refined olive oil, pomace oil, and seed oils have a lower flash point than virgin olive oil. Virgin olive oils have a flash point around 410° to 428°F (210° to 220°C), while most seed oils begin to burn at 374° to 392°F (190° to 200°C). Different than smoke point.

- **Metal traces:** A measure of the amount of iron and copper in a sample taken by burning the oil in a special high-temperature graphite oven and analyzing the ash with atomic absorption.

- **Halogenated solvents:** A measure of the quantity of chloroform, trichloroethylene, and tetrachloroethylene that may be present as residuals in solvent-extracted oils. Headspace volatile gases are measured in a gas chromatograph and expressed in milligrams per kilogram (mg/kg).

- **Additives:** For virgin olive oils none are permitted. For refined olive oil, olive oil, refined pomace oil, and pomace oil a maximum of 200 milligrams per kilogram of alpha-tocopherol is permitted.

- **Heavy metals and pesticide residues:** All oils must comply with Codex Alimentarius maximum limits.

- **Sterol composition and content:** Sterols are important components of the nonglycerin fraction of olive oil. Their presence is determined by gas chromatography. Refined olive oils and or pomace oils have higher total sterol levels and specific sterol types must also be within certain maximum levels.

- **Fatty acid composition:** Measured by gas chromatography and can help distinguish between varieties and growing region, and also between some seed oils and olive oil. The basic percentages of fatty acid types are well documented for each oil within a certain range.

- **Saturated fatty acid content in position 2 of the triglyceride:** The middle carbon of the triglyceride molecule (2, or beta, position) in natural virgin olive oil always contains the nonsaturated fatty acids such as oleic or linoleic. Re-esterified oils that are processed artificially do not conform to this same fatty acid distribution and can be detected with gas chromatography.

- **Unsaponifiable material:** The content of components that would not turn to soap under the process of saponification (addition of lye). Limits must be within those specified.

- **Wax content:** Used to identify the presence of pomace oil and is determined by gas chromatography. Refining processes can more easily eliminate aliphatic alcohols, but waxes are more difficult to remove. The wax content is higher in pomace oil, because pomace contains a greater proportion of fruit skin where most of the waxes originate.

- **Erythrodiol and uvaol:** Two terpenic alcohols that can be detected with gas chromatography. Some secondary-extracted oils, refined pomace oil, and crude pomace oil can exceed the legal limit. Most of these compounds are found in the skin of the fruit.

- **ECN 42 content:** Seed oils can also be detected by the difference of equivalent carbon number (ECN) of the oil molecules determined by high performance liquid chromatography (HPLC) and the theoretical ECN calculated from fatty acid content. Trilinolein is a triglyceride molecule that is not naturally present in olive oil, but appears in seed oils, especially in sunflower oil. HPLC is used to detect this molecule that has the configuration of 3 linoleic fatty acids attached to glycerin (more double bonds); levels cannot exceed the percentages in each category.

- **Hydrocarbons:** Certain hydrocarbons such as stigmastadienes and the relationship of stigmasta-3, 5 diene, and campesta-3, 5 diene (R1) can be identified in refined olive oils that have been heated and decolorized. They are not present in virgin olive oil.

- **Transfatty acid isomer:** When oils are exposed to high heat or pressure they can change from the "cis" (natural) form to the "trans" form. Detection is made using gas chromatography. This method can also detect whether oil has been exposed to color removal substances. Transfat has been shown to raise "bad" LDL cholesterol, lower "good" HDL cholesterol, have adverse effects on the inner lining of blood vessels, and raises the risk of diabetes. Normal cis olive oil has fatty acid molecules that have a curved shape, which allows them to be metabolized properly. Heat and hydrogenation twists the shape (trans) so it does not "fit" correctly with enzymes. Beginning in 2006, new labeling laws in the United States require products to be labeled with the content of transfatty acids.

- **Total aliphatic alcohols:** Low in virgin olive oil, but much higher in solvent-extracted pomace oil, because their levels are higher in fruit skin. Aliphatic alcohol content is measured using gas chromatography. Extra virgin, virgin, and ordinary olive oils cannot exceed 250 mg/kg, lampante oil should be less than 400 mg/kg, and refined olive oil must be less than 350 mg/kg.

- **DNA characterization:** Recovery of intact or large fragments of DNA from the protein residue in olive oil by using electrophoresis and RAPD analysis to develop a fingerprint. This is the newest technology and a standard for it has not yet been developed.

．．

CALIFORNIA OLIVE OIL COUNCIL STANDARDS

A private membership organization of oil olive producers and processors in California called the California Olive Oil Council (COOC) has adopted the international standards and is promoting the adoption of these standards by the state and federal government. Consumers have become familiar with the international standard and nomenclature that most labels indicate, such as "Extra Virgin Olive Oil," "Virgin Olive Oil," or "Olive Oil." In order to set apart California olive oils that have met the international sensory, free fatty acid, and peroxide value standards, the COOC developed an "Extra Virgin Certification Seal" program. Each participant member of the COOC submits their oil along with laboratory test results completed for free acidity and peroxide value. The oil is tasted by a taste panel according to their standards. Oils that meet the criteria are promoted by the council at their events, in media releases, publicity materials, and through in-store promotions (plate 3.4).

In 1997, the California Legislature enacted a law amending Health and Safety Code § 112895 relating to truth in labeling olive oil as to location of production, processing, and bottling. Introduced as State Senate Bill 920, the law makes it a crime to sell imitation olive oil or to sell olive oil labeled as "California" olive oil that contains oil from any other source. It also specifies that oils labeled according to designated American-approved "viticultural areas" be composed of 75 percent of oil that is derived solely from olives grown in that designated American viticultural area. See the California State Senate Legislation Web site, http://info.sen.ca.gov/pub/97-98/bill/sen/sb_0901-0950/sb_920_bill_19970905_enrolled.html.

· ·

REFERENCES

Alba Mendoza, J., J. R. Izquierdo, and F. Gutiérrez Rosales. 1997. Aceite de plive virgen análisis sensorial. Madrid: Editorial Agrícola Española.

AOCS (American Oil Chemists Society). 1998. In D. Firestone, ed., Official methods and recommended practices of the AOCS. 5th ed. Urbana, IL: AOCS, http://www.aocs.org.

Carpio Dueñas, A., and B. Jiménez Herrera. 1993. Características organolépticas y análisis sensorial del aceite de oliva. 4th ed. Junta de Andalucía, ed. Sevilla: J. de Haro Ardes Gráficas, S. L. Parque Ind. P.I.S.A.

Harwood, J. L., and R. Aparicio. 2000. Handbook of olive oil: Analysis and properties. Gaitherburg, MD: Aspen Publishers.

IOOC (International Olive Oil Council). 1996a. General methodology for the organoleptic assessment of virgin olive oil. IOOC standard procedure COI/T.20/Doc. no. 13. Madrid, Spain.

———. 1996b. Organoleptic assessment of virgin olive oil. RES. COI/T.20/Doc. no. 15/Rev. 5. Madrid, Spain.

———. 1996c. Sensory analysis: General basic vocabulary. IOOC standard COI/T.20/Doc. no. 4. Madrid, Spain.

———. 1999. Trade standard applying to olive oil and olive pomace oil. RES. COI/T.15/NC no. 2/9 (revised June 10). Madrid, Spain.

———. 2003. Trade standard applying to olive oil and olive pomace oil. RES. COI/T.15/NC no. 3/Rev. 1 (Dec. 5). Madrid, Spain.

ISO (International Standards Organization). 2003. International standards catalogue: Standards for animal and vegetable fats and oils. 67.200. ISO Web site, http://www.iso.org/iso/en/CatalogueListPage.CatalogueList.

IUPAC (International Union of Pure and Applied Chemistry). 1992. Standard methods for the analysis of oils, fats, and derivatives. C. Paquot and A. Haufenne, eds. Oxford, UK: Blackwell.

Kiritsakis, A. K., E. B. Lenert, W. C. Willet, and R. J. Hernandez. 1998. Olive oil: From tree to table. 2nd ed. Trumbull, CT: Food and Nutrition Press.

Vossen, P. M. 2001. Producing olive oil. In G. S. Sibbett and L. Ferguson, eds., Olive production manual. 2nd ed. Oakland: University of California Agriculture and Natural Resources Publication 3353. 157–173.

4

California Olive Oil Industry Survey Statistics

PAUL M. VOSSEN AND ALEXANDRA KICENIK DEVARENNE

HISTORY AND INTRODUCTION

The Spanish missionary priests were the first in California to make olive oil from trees planted around their missions. Many of those missions still have some of the original Mission variety trees on the grounds, and some still have remnants of old mills. The first commercial olive oil production in California was from the Camulos mill in Ventura in 1871. By 1885, California olive growers were producing oil from approximately 2,000 acres (809 ha) and several mills, but the industry never increased to any significant size due to strong economic competition from European imports and seed oils.

The "California Style" firm, black olive was developed in the northern Sacramento Valley in the early 1900s and initiated a new planting boom with a combination of the old Mission variety and new table varieties such as Manzanillo, Ascolano, Sevillano (Gordal), and Barouni. The table fruit industry ultimately grew to over 35,000 acres (14,165 ha) with about 70 percent of the production in the southern San Joaquin Valley counties (Tulare 57 percent, Madera 8 percent, and Fresno 4 percent) and the remaining 30 percent in the northern Sacramento Valley counties (Tehama 15 percent, Glenn 11 percent, Butte 2 percent, and other foothill counties 2 percent). Most of these plantings were made at the traditional density of about 75 to 100 trees per acre (185 to 247 per ha). The olive oil industry existed for many years almost exclusively as a salvage operation for undersized or damaged table fruit. No new plantings of oil varieties occurred until 1990, when several small-scale producers in Northern California began to plant Italian varieties.

A new demand for olive oil in the high-quality "gourmet" olive oil prompted the planting of several small orchards and development of several new olive oil mills, first in the north coast counties of Napa, Sonoma, Alameda, Marin, Mendocino, and Lake. New small-scale plantings quickly spread to the south coast counties of San Luis Obispo, Monterey, and Santa Barbara. These orchards were planted primarily to Italian varieties such as Frantoio, Leccino, Pendolino, Taggiasca, and Coratina at high-density spacing ranging from 250 to 300 trees per acre (618 to 741 per ha).

There was a simultaneous rejuvenation of old, abandoned orchards in these same coastal counties, as well as in the Sierra Foothill counties of Calaveras, Nevada, Amador, and El Dorado. Some historians believe that there were approximately 2,000 acres (809 ha) of various unknown varieties planted in the more rugged parts of Napa and Sonoma Counties. At one time there were approximately 5,000 commercially viable acres (2,024 ha) of Mission variety trees in the foothill areas of Butte County; many remain semiabandoned or as pastureland and woods. It is estimated that hundreds of acres of old neglected trees from the late 1800s and early 1900s still exist in the Sierra foothills. Several smaller old plantings of olives can also be found throughout the southern California coastal area.

The most recent influence in the California olive oil industry started in 1999 with the planting of the first super-high-density orchard designed to accommodate over-the-row mechanical harvesters. Super-high-density-system trees are planted at a density of about 650 to 900 trees per acre (1,605 to 2,223 per ha), and the trees are maintained in a narrow hedgerow lower than 10 feet (3 m). This precipitated a significant planting boom of new orchards primarily in the Central Valley. These orchards use very specific clonal selections of Arbequina, Koroneiki, and Arbosana, which are low-vigor varieties that come into bearing early, are highly productive, and produce very high quality olive oils.

The University of California Cooperative Extension (UCCE) Farm Advisor's office in Sonoma County has conducted informal phone interviews of olive oil processors over the last 10 years to develop an idea of industry size and trends. Informal notations were also made on plantings or rejuvenated from conversations with county agricultural commission field staff and UCCE Farm Advisors throughout the state. Other trends have been noted in the number of commercial mills in operation and the increase of olive oil brands in the marketplace. Almost all of the information in the past about the California olive oil industry was generated from those estimates without conducting a formal survey.

The last 10 years have seen enormous change in the California olive oil industry. It has gone from a handful of producers to several hundred today. Most are small-scale producers, but some are very large, and there is interest in this crop statewide. Many new orchards have been planted, new varieties have been introduced from Europe, and several new processing plants have been established. The consumer has gone from a choice of relatively few California-produced olive oils to a large and varied selection of labels and styles.

The UCCE helped the industry develop a sensory taste panel to evaluate quality in compliance with the International Olive Oil Council (IOOC) standard (see chapter 3, "International Olive Oil Council Trade Standard for Olive Oil"). Many California producers are making excellent international-award-winning, quality oils now present at national food buyer shows. A recent *Consumer Reports* magazine article recognized two California olive oils as superior to several European oils.

....

SURVEY METHODOLOGY

The survey was designed to give as complete a picture of the industry as possible. It had three parts, addressing nurseries, growers, and processors. By sending all three parts to each person or company, we received information that might otherwise have been missed: an orchard at a business that is primarily a nursery, for example. The survey inquired about future plantings as well as those in the past. This survey followed University of California protocol regarding research involving human subjects. Information gathered in the survey was to remain anonymous and confidential, and the surveys were destroyed once the survey was completed. Finally, we contacted every known nonrespondent by phone, fax, or e-mail. This approach garnered a response from a very high percentage of the producers in California.

In any survey, the response by all the growers, processors, or nurseries is incomplete. There were a limited number of olive nurseries (17) and a small number of mills (27). Since all of them responded, we have a very high degree of confidence in the data generated from those sectors of the industry. We ultimately received data on all of the known olive oil growers in the state using lists provided by county agricultural commissioners and UCCE Farm Advisors. Some data is not complete, however, and had to be estimated, especially from the counties of Tulare, Glenn, Tehama, and Butte, because the amount of fruit that is diverted to oil from the table industry is so variable. In years when fruit prices are higher due to low crop volume and larger-sized fruit, virtually all fruit is processed as table fruit. In heavy cropping years, when prices are low, or when fruit is undersized or damaged by olive fruit fly, more gets diverted to oil processors.

We reached about three-fourths of the olive oil growers in those counties and estimated the missing numbers, acreage, and production figures based on cross-references with the amount of oil produced in the nearby mills. Based on gallons of oil produced, we calculated back to acreage and traditional fruit yields from those types of orchards and cultivars grown. In some areas a significant amount of oil is produced from fruit harvested by farm labor contractors seeking work in the winter months, when little else is available. We contacted some of them, but the response rate was poor. Estimates therefore were included for these orchards. Anecdotal evidence from numerous sources cited the existence of old, abandoned orchards throughout the state, but little reliable data was obtained regarding these orchards. Abandoned olive orchards may constitute as much as an additional 2,000 to 5,000 acres (809 to 2,024 ha) in California. Since these orchards are not harvested, they have not been included in our results.

....

PROCESSING MILLS

There are 27 operating mills of significant size in California, producing from 100 to over 100,000 gallons (3.785 to 3,785 hl) of olive oil annually. Most (60 percent) of these are very small processors producing less than 5,000 gallons (189 hl) per year and only 7 percent of the state's olive oil. The medium-size producers (18 percent) make between 5,000 and 15,000 gallons (189 and 568 hl) of oil per season and produce 13 percent of the state's olive oil. The bulk of the production, 80 percent, comes from the remaining 22 percent of the producers in their larger mills. California's 27 mills produced 247,550 gallons (9,370 hl) of olive oil in 1999–2000; 138,446 gallons (5,240 hl) in 2000–2001; 246,491 gallons (9,330 hl) in 2001–2002; 265,300 gallons (10,042 hl) in 2002–2003; 306,065

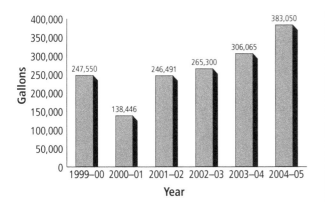

Figure 4.1. Annual olive oil production in California, 1999–2005. *Source:* Vossen and Devarenne 2005.

Table 4.1. California olive oil production

Year	Production (gal)	Production (hl)	Percent change
1996–97	123,000	4,656	—
1997–98	200,000	7,570	+ 62
1998–99	236,000	8,933	+ 18
1999–00	247,550	9,370	+ 5
2000–01	138,446	5,240	– 44
2001–02	246,491	9,330	+ 78
2002–03	265,300	10,042	+ 8
2003–04	306,065	11,585	+ 15
2004–05	383,050	14,498	+25

gallons (11,585 hl) in 2003–2004; and 383,050 gallons (14,498 hl) in 2004–2005 (fig. 4.1).

Olive oil production in California has increased by an average of 20 percent per year over the last 9 years. The only year that there was a decline in production was in 2000–2001 due to a statewide reduction in crop caused by poor weather conditions in an "off" alternate bearing year. Production the following year (2001–2002) showed the largest single-year increase of 78 percent above the previous year (table 4.1). Production should continue to increase each year until 2009–2010 or later as nonbearing acreage comes into production.

· ·

GROWERS

As of 2005, there were 528 reported California olive oil growers in 38 California counties. The number of growers in each county ranges from 1 to 114. The top eight counties have 52 percent of the growers, so the numbers are fairly evenly split over most of the remaining counties. The average number of growers per county is 14. The counties with the most growers are Sonoma (114), Napa (75), San Luis Obispo (27), Mendocino (18), Butte (18), Amador (16), Marin (14), and Lake (10) (fig. 4.2). Growers in these eight counties represent 42 percent of the states' acreage and 50 percent of the oil. Dividing up the 38 counties reporting olive oil production into six geographic regions provides an interesting perspective on how the amount of production and number of growers are situated within the state of California (table 4.2).

The North Coast (Alameda, Contra Costa, Lake, Marin, Mendocino, Napa, Santa Clara, and Sonoma Counties) has the largest number of growers 268 (51 percent) and 1,535 acres, or 621 hectares (25 percent), with the smallest average olive orchard size at 5 acres (2 ha). This area has 18 percent of the state's 2004–05

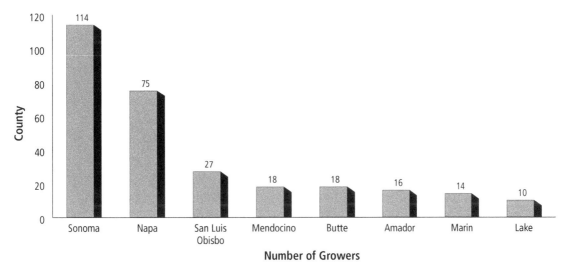

Figure 4.2. California counties with the greatest number of olive oil growers, 2004. *Source:* Vossen and Devarenne 2005.

Table 4.2. California olive oil grower statistics by region, 2005

Region	Number of growers	Percentage of total growers	Acreage	Average size (ac)	Range	Percentage of total acres	Percentage of total production
North Coast	268	51	1,535	5	1–175	24.9	18
Central Coast	59	11	376	6	1–40	6.1	3
South Coast and Southern California	17	3	70	14	1–20	1.1	1
Sacramento Valley	94	18	3,216	30	1–450	52.1	54
San Joaquin Valley	39	7	707	23	1–245	11.5	21
Sierra Foothills	51	10	264	8	1–50	4.3	3
Total	**528**	**100**	**6,168**	**14**	**1–450**	**100**	**100**

Note: For metric conversion, 1 acre = 0.4047 hectares.

production, and most of the orchards are nonbearing or just starting to come into production. The vast majority of the orchards are planted to Italian varieties such as Frantoio, Leccino, and Pendolino in the high-density system, with 250 to 300 trees per acre (618 to 741 per ha). Many wineries also have small olive plantings for oil, often incorporated into landscaping.

The Central Coast (Monterey, San Benito, San Luis Obispo, and Santa Barbara Counties) has 59 growers (11 percent) and 376 acres (152 ha) in oil olives, which is 6 percent of California's acreage and 3 percent of the oil production of 2004–05. Its characteristics are similar to the North Coast, with an average orchard size of 6 acres (2.4 ha).

The South Coast and Southern California (Los Angeles, Riverside, San Diego, and Ventura Counties) has 17 growers (3 percent) and 70 acres (28 ha), which is 1 percent of the state's olive oil acreage with an average size of 14 acres (5.7 ha) each and 1 percent of the production of 2004–2005.

The Sacramento Valley (Butte, Glenn, Sacramento, San Joaquin, Shasta, Solano, Sutter, Tehama, Yolo, and Yuba Counties) has 94 growers (18 percent), with the largest number of acres (3,217, or 1,302 ha), which is about half (52 percent) of California's land planted to oil olives with the largest average-size farms. It also produces over half of the states' olive oil (54 percent). This is traditionally an olive-growing area, with many old widely spaced orchards of 100 trees per acre (247/ ha) planted to Mission, Ascolano, Sevillano, and Manzanillo varieties. It was also the first region to plant orchards in the super-high-density system, 650 to 900 trees per acre (1,605 to 2,223 per ha) with Arbequina, Arbosana, and Koroneiki varieties. Some of those orchards are now in full production.

The San Joaquin Valley (Fresno, Madera, Merced, San Joaquin, Stanislaus, and Tulare Counties) has 39 growers (7 percent), 707 acres, or 286 ha (11 percent)

of the acreage, and 21 percent of the production. This region has the second-largest average-size orchard, with several new growers that have planted super-high-density orchards.

The Sierra Foothills (Amador, Calaveras, El Dorado, Nevada, Placer, and Tuolumne Counties) has 51 growers (10 percent), 264 acres, or 107 ha (4 percent), and 3 percent of California's production. This region has a mix of many widely spaced, small-scale orchards of old varieties and small new plantings of primarily Italian varieties.

The top eleven olive oil producing counties by gallonage are shown in figure 4.3. These counties represent 75 percent of California's total olive oil production (383,050 gallons, or 14,998 hectoliters) and have 19 of the 27 major processing mills. The leading county is Butte with 124,000 gallons (4,693 hl) of oil production followed by Tulare with 39,000 gallons (1,476 hl), Tehama with 25,500 gallons (965 hl), Glenn with 21,000 gallons (795 hl), Sonoma with 17,950 gallons (679 hl), Marin with 17,500 gallons (662 hl), Alameda with 10,500 gallons (397 hl), Napa with 9,870 gallons (374 hl), San Joaquin with 9,500 gallons (360 hl), Fresno with 8,500 gallons (322 hl), and San Luis Obispo with 2,400 gallons (91 hl) of oil produced in 2004–2005. The leading olive-oil-producing counties have many mature table fruit variety orchards in full production that have traditionally provided a significant amount of California's olive oil. Butte County was also the first to plant significant acreage into the super-high-density system, which is reflected in its production.

In 2004, California had 6,168 acres (2,496 ha) in oil olives. Figure 4.4 shows the top 12 olive oil producing counties by acreage in California. Butte County, with 1,553 acres (628 ha), and Tehama, with 979 acres (396 ha), have old mature orchards as well as significant new acreage planted to the super-high-

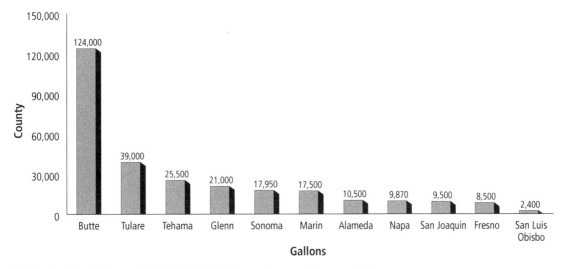

Figure 4.3. Top olive-oil-producing counties in California, 2004. *Source:* Vossen and Devarenne 2005.

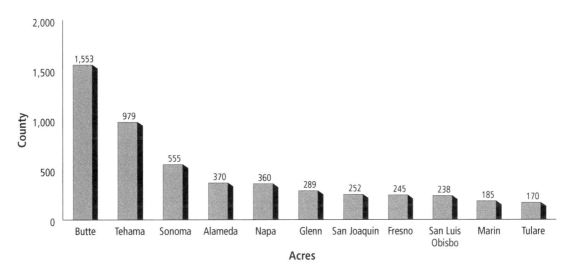

Figure 4.4. Top olive-oil-producing counties in California by acreage, 2004. *Source:* Vossen and Devarenne 2005.

density system. Sonoma County, with 555 acres (225 ha), Alameda, with 370 acres (148 ha), and Napa, with 360 acres (146 ha), have many newly planted orchards that are nonbearing or just beginning to come into production, planted primarily with Italian varieties in the high-density system. Many are associated with wineries. Glenn County, with 289 acres (117 ha), has mostly mature table olive orchards reported as currently being harvested for processing into oil. San Joaquin, with 252 acres (102 ha), and Fresno, with 245 acres (99 ha), have small plantings of old, mature table olive orchards, some of which go to oil production, but most of the acreage is newly planted super-high-density orchards. San Luis Obispo County, with 238 acres (96 ha), is mostly planted to Italian varieties, and most of those orchards are just coming into pro-

duction. Marin County, with 185 acres (75 ha), has mostly newly planted orchards that are still nonbearing or just coming into full production. Most of those orchards are planted to Italian varieties.

Tulare County has 170 reported acres (69 ha) for oil production. This is primarily a table fruit producing area, with most of the acreage in Manzanillo variety trees. The amount of fruit diverted to oil varies from year to year depending on the table fruit market.

Of all the 6,168 olive oil acres (2,496 ha) reported in 2004, 66 percent are classified as organic and 34 percent as conventionally grown. The organic production can be broken down into 16 percent certified organic, 9 percent in transition to certified organic, and 41 percent being grown with organic methods but without certification.

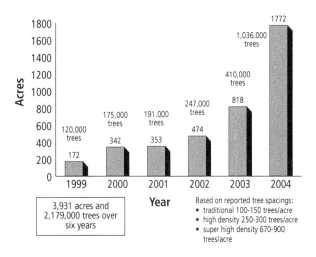

Figure 4.5. Number of olive oil trees sold by California nurseries and equivalent acreage, 1999–2004. *Source:* Vossen and Devarenne 2005.

....

NURSERIES

Seventeen nurseries' responses constituted this survey. These represent all of the significant tree sales in California. There are about 2.75 million oil olive trees in California, and most, 2.18 million, were planted after 2000. Prior to 1990, most acreage was planted at the traditional 100 to 150 trees per acre (247 to 370 per ha). Since then, about half of the new acreage has been planted at high densities, 250 to 300 trees per acre (618 to 741 per ha), and the other half at super high densities, 650 to 900 trees per acre (1,605 to 2,223 per ha) (fig. 4.5).

The following acreage figures are calculated mathematically from the number of trees reported sold each year and the indicated tree spacings by variety. Based on that conversion, there were an estimated 3,931 acres (1,595 ha) planted from 1999 to 2004. These newly planted trees comprise 64 percent of the total acreage in California. About 70 percent of that new acreage is still nonbearing or just starting to come into production. This means that the amount of oil produced in California could easily double within the next 5 to 7 years. The estimated 1,700 to 2,000 acres (688 to 809 ha) of super-high-density orchards planted over the last 6 years will come into production very quickly. The 1,940 acres (785 ha) of lower-density orchards will take 5 years or so to reach full production. There are also another 2,000 acres (809 ha) of new plantings planned for 2005, mostly in the Sacramento and San Joaquin Valleys.

The varieties of olive trees planted in California have changed dramatically over the last 6 years. Prior to 1999 most of the trees were table varieties (Mission and Manzanillo) and Italian varieties (Frantoio, Leccino, and Pendolino), but the last 6 and particularly the last 3 years have been dominated by Spanish varieties (Arbequina and Arbosana) and the Greek variety (Koroneiki) suitable for super-high-density planting. The top ten varieties planted in California over the last six years from 1999 to 2004 were Arbequina with 1,089,900 trees planted on 1,626 acres (658 ha); Arbosana, with 173,850 trees planted on 260 acres (105 ha); Frantoio, with 118,830 trees planted on 400 acres (162 ha); Mission with 76,480 trees planted on 510 acres (206 ha); Koroneiki, with 73,550 trees planted on 110 acres (45 ha); Leccino, with 65,461 trees planted on 220 acres (89 ha); Manzanillo, with 58,200 trees planted on 545 acres (221 ha); Pendolino, with 30,118 trees planted on 100 acres (40 ha); Taggiasca with 15,250 trees planted on 50 acres (20 ha); and Coratina, with 11,232 trees planted on 40 acres (16 ha) (fig. 4.6).

....

CONCLUSION

Since 1996, the production of California olive oil has increased by 168 percent. From 1999 to 2004, close to 4,000 acres (1,619 ha) of olives have been planted specifically for oil. When those trees come into full production in the next 5 to 7 years California could easily be producing 750,000 gallons (28,388 hl) of olive oil annually. The trend towards larger-scale, super-high-density plantings could drive the number of gallons up more quickly, because of the relatively short time those orchards take to reach full production. At 750,000 gallons per year, California would equal France in olive oil production in the world.

The California olive oil industry, at 6,168 acres (2,496 ha), is small compared to the major agricultural crops in the state, but when compared to smaller specialty crops like winter pears, kiwis, or fresh market cucumbers, olive oil acreage is similar. Due to the high added value of oil processing, the economic picture is even better. If each gallon of California olive oil sells for $22.50 in the bulk market, that would be a value of almost $17 million, and quite similar to winter pears, kiwis, and figs. If retail prices are used for bottled olive oil at $113 per gallon based on 500-ml bottles at $15.00 per bottle, the value of the California olive oil industry would be $84,750,000. As California's reputation for excellence in olive oil grows in the domestic and international markets, the demand will likely increase. The significant new plantings shown by this survey will be increasing the state's production in the immediate future to meet such a demand.

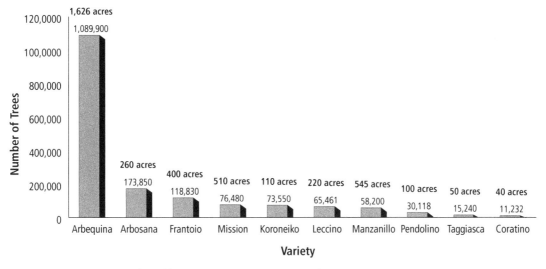

Figure 4.6. Top ten olive varieties planted in California, 1999–2004. *Source:* Vossen and Devarenne 2005.

ACKNOWLEDGMENT

Thank you to the Burton D. Morgan Foundation for their support for this survey-research project. Their support has benefited the entire California olive oil industry.

REFERENCES

Connell, J. H. 2004. History and scope of the olive industry. In G. S. Sibbett and L. Ferguson, eds., Olive production manual. 2nd ed. Oakland: University of California Agriculture and Natural Resources Publication 3353. 1–10.

Consumer Reports. 2004. Olive oil: A cheap bottle beats a pricier lineup. 69(9): 32–35.

Vossen, P. M., and A. Devarenne. 2005. California olive oil industry survey statistics. UC Cooperative Extension Sonoma County Web site, http://cesonoma.ucdavis.edu/hortic/pdf/survey_olive_oil_in_ca_05.pdf.

California Olive Oil Industry Statistics Update

There has been a significant increase in plantings of olives specifically for oil production since the 2004 UC survey. At that time the survey snapshot put California's production at 6,168 acres (2,496 ha). In 2005 and 2006 (occurring that summer and fall) there was a documented increase of 3,870 acres (1,566 ha) in super-high-density plantings alone. Those plantings were almost exclusively Arbequina, Arbosana, and Koroneiki. Another estimated 500 acres (202 ha) of standard-density orchards were to have been planted, primarily to Frantoio, Leccino, and Pendolino. This means that by fall 2006, the total estimated acres of oil olives was 10,500 (4,249 ha), an increase of about 70 percent. In that same period, table olive acreage declined by about 3,000 acres (1,214 ha). Most of the new plantings of oil olives are occurring in Butte, Glenn, San Joaquin, and San Luis Obispo Counties in farms over 100 acres (40 ha) in size. One orchard in Glenn County, scheduled to be planted in August 2006, will be 800 acres (324 ha). Growers are optimistic that with the competitive advantage of mechanical harvest, a huge domestic market, and excellent quality they will be able to compete well against imported oils. An additional 11 new and significantly upgraded mils have also been or are being installed in California over the last two years.

Source: First Press (UCCE Newsletter of Olive Oil Production and Evaluation), vol. 1 no. 4 (Summer 2006): 1. See the UCCE Sonoma County Web site, http://cesonoma.ucdavis.edu/.

Part 2
Nutrition for Organic Olive Orchards

5

Organic Olive Orchard Nutrition

JOSEPH H. CONNELL AND PAUL M. VOSSEN

In order to grow well and produce an acceptable economic return, olives must have adequate nutrition. Unlike many other fruit and vegetable crops, olive trees are not heavy feeders. They have been cultivated for thousands of years and are hardy, tough plants that tolerate poor growing conditions—especially low fertility—better than most other fruit trees. Deep, fertile soils, important for good growth and production for other orchard crops, may actually be a negative factor for olives. In very fertile soils, irrigation and nutrition must be managed to avoid excessive vegetative growth and resulting light bloom and fruit set. The crop from such trees often produces lower-quality oil, especially if high vigor is combined with luxuriant irrigation and good weed control practices.

Olive trees tend to bloom and fruit more consistently under conditions of moderate vigor with minimal but adequate nutrition, as long as no critical element is deficient. High nitrogen (N) can improve growth in low-vigor sites, but it can result in excessive growth in others. Low potassium (K) has been observed to cause

olive trees to be more susceptible to cold and drought. If severe, low potassium can also cause defoliation and twig dieback. A lack of the minor element boron (B) has been shown to limit fruit set and can have a negative effect on fruit development. Excess boron stunts tree growth. Olive trees can also tolerate a very wide pH range that may affect the uptake of phosphorus (P), calcium (Ca), magnesium (Mg), and potassium.

A common mistake often made by new olive growers when trees are not growing adequately is to respond with heavy fertilizer or compost applications when the trees are really lacking other basic cultural needs such as adequate water and good weed control. There is a myth that good nutrition will prevent diseases or insect attacks, improve yield, and provide better quality olives or olive oil. In fact, just the opposite may be true. Once trees have adequate nutrition, additional applications of fertilizer or compost are an unnecessary cost and a practice that can lead to environmental pollution.

In order for the orchard to come into full production quickly it is very important to adequately fertilize young trees so that they grow rapidly to fill their space in the orchard. The rates of fertilizers specified here are for mature trees; for young trees, the rates should be multiplied by the canopy percentage of a full-sized tree. For example, a 3-year-old orchard with only 10 percent full canopy coverage would receive just 10 percent of the fertilizer rate of a mature orchard.

Table 5.1. Critical nutrient levels in olive leaves from tissue analysis (leaf samples taken in July)

Element	Deficient	Sufficient	Toxic
nitrogen (N) (%)	1.40	1.50–2.00	—
phosphorus (P) (%)	—	0.10–0.30	—
potassium (K) (%)	0.40	> 0.80	—
calcium (Ca) (%)	—	> 1.00	—
magnesium (Mg) (%)	—	> 0.10	—
manganese (Mn) (ppm)	—	> 20	—
copper (Cu) (ppm)	—	> 4	—
boron (B) (ppm)	14	19–150	185
sodium (Na) (%)	—	—	> 0.20
chlorine (Cl) (%)	—	—	> 0.50

Source: Beutel et al. 1983.

Note: Zinc deficiency has not been observed in California olives.

DIAGNOSING NUTRIENT DEFICIENCIES

There are 16 known essential nutrients for good plant growth. Sufficient levels have been determined for the nutrients shown in table 5.1. Of these, only nitrogen, potassium, and boron are ever likely to require supplemental applications in California. Potassium and boron deficiencies are relatively rare.

Sidebar 5.1
Benefits of organic matter

- Aids water infiltration.
- Develops soil structure.
- Provides larger reservoir for nitrogen and other micronutrients.
- Slow release of nutrients.

Sidebar 5.2
Challenges with higher organic matter

- Larger reservoir for nitrogen must be managed year-round or nitrates can be leached to groundwater or can run off.
- If cover crop is grown, the orchard may require additional water.
- May provide excess nitrogen.

There are two methods of determining the nutritional status of olive trees, and they work best when applied simultaneously. The primary method is to use tissue analysis to measure the chemical composition of the leaves. This involves taking approximately 100 fully developed leaves per sample from the middle of nonbearing current-season shoots in July and sending them to a reputable laboratory for analysis. If a nutrient is lacking or below a specified sufficient level, there may be a deficiency in the soil, or there may be another reason why it is not being taken up. There are well-established guidelines for nutrient levels for olives (see table 5.1). Soil analysis is not accurate enough to be used to diagnose fertility needs in olives, but it is useful for determining pH or diagnosing salt problems.

The second method for determining the nutritional status of the trees is to become familiar with and watch for visual deficiency symptoms on the leaves and fruit. Trees with very low nitrogen levels have leaves with a light green to yellow tinge and poor shoot growth (see plate 5.1). This symptom often occurs during the winter when nitrogen is not as readily available in cold, wet, heavy soils, but it may disappear completely as soils warm and root activity increases in the early summer. Phosphorus deficiency is extremely rare (unknown in California), and it appears as very small leaves with purple coloration. A lack of potassium first appears as leaf tip yellowing on older leaves (see plate 5.4). When severe, the leaf tips die, turn brown, and the leaves fall off, followed by twig dieback within the tree. Symptoms like this may also appear due to other problems such as poor soil drainage. Like nitro-

gen deficiency, potassium deficiency may be transient, first showing up in the winter or spring particularly in wet years and then disappearing as the weather warms and soil conditions more favorable for nutrient uptake develop. Boron deficiency shows up as misshapen fruit, short branch growth, twig dieback, rough bark, and leaves with a yellow band between brown leaf tips and the green leaf base (see plates 5.5 and 5.6). It is a relatively rare deficiency found sporadically in Sierra foothill regions.

FERTILIZING TREES ORGANICALLY

Organic materials provide the benefit of releasing their nutrients slowly but continuously throughout the year (sidebar 5.1). The disadvantage of this slow release of nutrients is that the trees cannot be manipulated quickly to stimulate growth or correct deficiencies when heavy crops are set. In addition, since nutrients are released constantly, nutrient loss to leaching or surface water runoff is a potential problem during the cold rainy season when trees are not actively taking up nutrients. This must be acknowledged and managed (sidebar 5.2).

To conform to USDA certified organic status and to be able to use the word "organic" on the olive oil or table olive label, only recognized organic fertilizers may be applied. Growers can find a list of products that comply with the law at the Organic Materials Review Institute (OMRI), http://www.omri.org. The Institute maintains a national list that specifies all synthetic substances allowed for use in organic production, all nonsynthetic substances prohibited for use in organic production, and all nonorganic ingredients permitted for use in handling and processing organic products. Before any product is used in an organic orchard the grower should always check with the organic certifier to be sure they will sign off on its use.

NITROGEN

A lack of nitrogen is the only common nutritional deficiency in olives. Most commercial olive growers apply only nitrogen, which easily corrects the common symptoms (sidebar 5.3 and plate 5.1). Organic nitrogen fertilizers from plant and animal waste products contain nitrogen in the form of amino acids and protein, which when added to the soil must be decomposed and then mineralized by soil macro- and microorganisms into ammonium and nitrate that plants can absorb and use.

Organic nitrogen fertilizers range in nitrogen concentration from about 0.5 to 12 percent. Nitrogen can be applied using organic materials such as feather or blood meal (plate 5.2), compost, or a leguminous cover crop. Rates of application should be in the range of about 40 to 100 pounds per acre (44.8 to 112 kg/ha) of actual nitrogen per year in a mature orchard, taking into account the percentage of nitrogen in the fertilizer (table 5.2).

The important thing about organic nitrogen fertility is to make applications in accordance with leaf analysis and to achieve adequate annual shoot growth of from 8 to 20 inches (20 to 51 cm) to ensure subsequent cropping potential. Nitrogen may not need to be applied every year. Carryover in the soil may last for several years, especially in heavy clay. In sandy soils, nitrates can leach and contribute to groundwater pollution. Applications made early in the growing season when trees are actively absorbing the nitrogen help minimize this potential.

Organic Nitrogen Materials

Organic fertilizers such as compost can take time to decompose and release their nitrogen in a form that the plants can absorb (plate 5.3). They decompose over about a 15-year period, with most of their nitrogen released within the first year or two. For whatever organic fertilizer is used, the amount of material applied should be related to the total nitrogen concentration in the material and to its nitrogen release rate (table 5.3). The amount applied should reflect the tree's needs and the availability of nitrogen from both current and previous applications. Annual applications over many years can build up high nitrogen levels. Considering that most compost contains about 2 percent nitrogen, the appropriate application rate would be about 1 to 2 tons per acre (2.24 to 4.48 T/ha) per year.

Concentrated organic fertilizers that are higher in nitrogen, such as feather meal or blood meal, are effective materials to use. They release their nitrogen much more quickly and are considerably more expen-

---

Sidebar 5.3
Low nitrogen symptoms

- Small, yellowish leaves
- Poor shoot growth
- Sporadic bloom
- Poor fruit set

---

sive, but they may be less costly to apply. Their normal nitrogen concentration is about 6 to 10 percent, so these materials should be applied at a rate of about 400 to 1,650 pounds per acre (448 to 1,848 kg/ha). There is mined, high-nitrogen, organic fertilizer from natural deposits in Chile (sodium nitrate) that is about 16 percent nitrate nitrogen, but it also contains sodium, which can be harmful to the trees. The practical use of this fertilizer is limited to soils having low sodium, where the profile is easily leached in a high rainfall climate.

Biologically Fixed Nitrogen: Legumes

Leguminous cover crops that naturally fix nitrogen from the air can be grown to supply all, most, or even too much of an olive orchard's needs. Bell beans and vetch that are commonly seeded in the fall and tilled into the soil in the spring can fix as much as 200 pounds per acre (224 kg/ha) of nitrogen. Clovers and

Table 5.2. Total nitrogen (N) concentration of selected soil amendments

Amendment	Total N concentration (%)
chicken manure compost	1.0–2.0
composted fresh grass clippings	1.0–2.0
dairy manure compost	0.5–1.5
beef manure compost	0.5–1.0
sheep manure compost	0.5–1.0
horse manure compost	0.5–1.0
composted woody materials	0.5–1.0

Table 5.3. Nitrogen (N) release rate of selected amendments

Amendment	Total N concentration (%)	Percentage of the total N released per year		
		1st year	2nd year	3rd year
chicken manure compost	2.0	30	15	10
animal manure compost	1.5	25	12	8
animal manure compost	1.0	20	10	5
compost: grass clippings	2.0	30	15	10
compost: woody materials	1.0	15	8	5

other legumes that are mowed will likely contribute only about 25 to 30 pounds per acre (28 to 33.6 kg/ha) of nitrogen as clippings decompose. Rainfall or sprinkling shortly after mowing helps incorporate nitrogen from the clippings back into the soil. Many organic growers have planted a subterranean clover cover crop that comes back from seed every year. They mow it and find that it provides most of the orchard's nitrogen needs without an excess. They can then supplement with applications of other materials if needed. Since the breakdown of a cover crop into amino acids and subsequently into mineral nitrogen for plant uptake is slower than conventional fertilizer applications, advanced planning is necessary. If necessary, applications of composts or dried concentrated forms of organic fertilizers such as feather meal, blood meal, fish waste, and so on can be concentrated around the root zone to boost growth, especially in young trees. These forms of nitrogen will still take several weeks in warm weather or several months in cool weather to provoke a response from the trees.

POTASSIUM

Potassium fertilizers are almost all mined from natural sources, and most are classified as organic. Conventional and organic potassium fertilizers are made directly from mined deposits high in potash. Composts and various animal waste products also contain small amounts of potassium. Potassium fertilizers can range from a concentration of about 0.5 to 60 percent. If a deficiency is noted (sidebar 5.4 and plate 5.4), a

mined source of potassium sulfate is usually applied to the soil in December to January at a rate of 10 to 20 pounds (4.5 to 9.1 kg) per tree, or about 500 to 1,000 pounds per acre (560 to 1,120 kg/ha) of potassium sulfate. The smaller amount is appropriate for sandy or lighter-textured soils, while the larger amount is required on heavier soils.

It is important that potassium materials be applied in bands alongside the tree row or in a ring around the tree just inside the drip line. Do not broadcast potassium. It is tied up by the soil and must be concentrated in bands to overcome the soil's ability to fix it and make it unavailable to the tree. In a cultivated orchard, bands should be shanked in to the depth of typical cultivations to be most effective. A shank is a tractor implement that cuts into the soil from 8 to 18 inches deep and places the fertilizer below the ground surface at a specified depth. Soil-applied potassium may require a year or two for tree response to become evident. In a nontilled orchard the bands can be applied to the soil surface. The correction is generally good for 3 to 5 years and sometimes longer.

The placement of the band applications should be recorded, and subsequent applications in future years should be made in the same location to avoid having to overcome new soil fixation. In drip-irrigated orchards applications can be made directly under emitters at about 20 percent of the banded rates, or the material can be dissolved and applied with the water.

When potassium is notably deficient, a foliar spray of 10 pounds potassium nitrate per 100 gallons (5.88 kg per 500 l) of water applied in the spring can be effective. Composts and other organic fertilizers contain some potassium, so regular concentrated applications in the tree row may help avoid a deficiency on some soils. On deficient soils, supplemental band applications are required to correct current and prevent future deficiency symptoms.

BORON

Boron is deficient in olives below 14 parts per million (ppm), adequate at 19 to 150 ppm, and in excess if over 185 ppm. Boron deficiency (plates 5.5 and 5.6) has been observed in olives on shallow foothill soils but could also be a problem on very sandy soils (sidebar 5.5 and plates 5.5 and 5.6). It is corrected by broadcasting 0.5 to 1 pound (227 to 454 g) of a 14- to 20-percent boron material per tree, or 25 to 50 pounds per acre (28 to 56 kg/ha) on the soil surface within the drip line during winter. One treatment will last several years. Be very careful not to apply too much boron since toxicity can occur.

When foliar analysis indicates low boron, a foliar spray of 7 ounces of borax per 100 gallons of water (262 g per 500 l) rapidly corrects the deficiency for that season. Applications of boron to trees prior to flower bud initiation or immediately prior to flowering has significantly improved fruit set even in trees with no visible symptoms and low, but not deficient, leaf boron levels.

....

OTHER NUTRIENTS

Phosphorus deficiency is presently unknown in California olives. If ever discovered to be deficient, phosphorus-containing fertilizers can be applied in either the conventional form or mineral form that conforms to USDA organic standards. Organic phosphate fertilizers are made from mined deposits that are high in phosphorus, but they are not treated with acids. Composts and various animal waste products also contain small amounts of phosphorus. Organic phosphorus fertilizers can range in concentration from about 0.5 to 7 percent; most are about 2 percent.

Nutrients such as zinc (Zn), copper (Cu), manganese (Mn), calcium, and magnesium have never been observed to be deficient in California olives. It is a waste of money and potentially polluting to apply these materials to olives. When nutrient deficiencies occur the correct approach is to determine exactly what is deficient and then apply specific corrective measures. Your local UC Cooperative Extension Farm Advisor, along with a reputable commercial agricultural analytical laboratory, can help identify nutrient deficiencies through a July leaf analysis.

....

APPLYING OLIVE OIL MILL WASTE

Olive mill waste can be used as a fertilizer just like any other organic material, but it must be handled carefully to avoid environmental contamination. Small to medium amounts of either liquid (fruit-water or wastewater) or solids (pomace) applied in dry weather are no problem. Problems can arise if large quantities or even small amounts are applied in rainy weather. Olive waste products contain large amounts of water-soluble organic compounds and can contaminate surface water systems by starving the water of oxygen as they break down. The solution is to add the wastewater or pomace to some type of dry bulking agent and hold it until it can be applied back onto the land during the spring or summer. If it composts in that process, it is not a problem; however, it is not necessary. Certainly, the composting process will make the nitrogen compounds more stable, but much will also be lost to ammonia volatilization. Olive pomace has a carbon to nitrogen ratio of about 30:1, so it will not compost without the addition of a high-nitrogen material. The addition of chicken or dairy manure at a rate of about 3:1 will help promote a very slow decomposition.

Olive wastewater effluent contains a useful array of mineral salts, but also some sodium. There have been no negative effects observed when this effluent is applied to row middles away from direct contact with the trees at rates of less than about 20,000 gallons per acre (187,200 l/ha). The difficulty is in storing it during the wet winter months when it is not needed for irrigation. Care must be taken to ensure that it does not spill into waterways or create odor problems. Wastewater should be used with great caution on areas with salt buildup, areas with low pH (unless lime is applied to moderate the pH effect), lands that already have excess nutrient accumulations, or sensitive crops that might suffer phytotoxic effects from the phenolic compounds or become damaged by temporary nitrogen deficiency. Most compost facilities need to add water at certain times of the year to keep the piles moist. Since this material contains nutrients that would help decompose cellulose and a high content of fermentable substances, water can be a beneficial addition to drying compost piles.

....

ORCHARD FLOOR MANAGEMENT

In olive orchards, the middles between the rows usually have a vegetative cover that is mowed (plate 5.7). Competing plant growth of any kind should be kept away from young trees to help ensure their rapid establishment. In mature orchards, a cover crop or resident vegetation is allowed to grow near the trees in many cases. As mature trees obtain a good balance between vegetative vigor and fruiting, ground covers growing near the trees may no longer provide significant competition. Most of the time with larger trees, that area becomes quite shaded and ground cover growth will be thin and greatly reduced.

Selected annual or perennial cover crops can be planted between rows in olive orchards, or the resident vegetation can be allowed to grow if it does not contain problematic weeds. In olives, an orchard floor covering can offer the advantages of a better surface for equipment access, possible nitrogen fixation, improved water infiltration, growth of roots in the most nutrient-rich surface soil, and a reduction in soil erosion. The disadvantages of leaving resident vegetation or establishing an orchard floor cover crop are that

- it may be cooler and increase damage by frost

- it may improve the survival of pests like olive fruit fly, olive peacock spot, gophers, rabbits, or mice

- it increases water usage in the orchard

- if it is not a legume, it will likely use some nitrogen

The orchard floor ground cover is usually mowed as needed, but it can be cultivated as well to save water in nonirrigated orchards or to open up silty soils that tend to seal over time without cultivation. The first decision that must be made is whether the area between the tree rows will be mowed or cultivated. Nontillage with a mowed cover generally takes less energy to farm and has more advantages than cultivation.

···

COVER CROPS

The following are some of the more commonly used cover crops and a brief description of their management for oil olive orchards..

Winter Annual Grasses (Mowed)

- **Zorro fescue (*Vulpia myuros* var. *hirsuta*).** This is a short-growing, very fine-bladed grass that reseeds well. It produces seed early in the spring so does not significantly increase water use. Mow after seeds are mature Seed at 10 to 20 pounds per acre (11.2 to 22.4 kg/ha).

- **Blando brome (*Bromus hordeaceus* spp. *molliformis*).** Also called soft chess, this is an intermediate-height grass that is more aggressive than Zorro fescue. It matures early and uses little water. Seed at 6 to 12 pounds per acre (6.7 to 13.4 kg/ha).

- **Annual ryegrass (*Lolium multiflorum*).** Annual ryegrass is a very aggressive, easy-to-establish grass that matures late and uses considerable water. It is very good in areas where erosion control is the primary consideration. Seed at 10 to 20 pounds per acre (11.2 to 22.4 kg/ha).

- **Grain, barley (*Hordeum vulgare*) and oat (*Avena sativa*).** These grow 3 feet (1 m) tall and compete well with weeds. They produce a large biomass. Mow and move forage to tree rows to reduce summer weeds. Seed at 60 to 90 pounds per acre (67.2 to 100.8 kg/ha).

Winter Annual Legumes (Mowed)

- **Subterranean clover (*Trifolium subterraneum*).** Many varieties exist. This low-growing (12 inches, or 31 cm) clover not only tolerates mowing but also successfully competes with weeds when mowed. It reseeds readily, matures early in the spring, and uses little water. Plant several varieties to assure a good stand. Seed at 12 to 20 pounds per acre (13.4 to 22.4 kg/ha).

- **Rose clover (*Trifolium hirtum*).** This low-growing (12 inches, or 31 cm) clover sets seed early and uses little water. Several varieties exist. Seed at 9 to 12 pounds per acre (10.1 to 13.4 kg/ha).

- **Crimson clover (*Trifolium incarnatum*).** This clover grows about 18 inches (46 cm) tall and is slightly more aggressive than subterranean or rose clover. It matures later and reseeds only under high moisture conditions. Seed at 9 to 12 pounds per acre (10.1 to 13.4 kg/ha).

- **Bur clover (*Medicago polymorpha*).** This native medic clover can be mowed short. It reseeds early with little water use. Seed at 6 to 10 pounds per acre (6.7 to 11.2 kg/ha).

- **Berseem clover (*Trifolium alexandrinum*).** This 14- to 18-inch (36- to 46-cm) clover produces more biomass than the other annual clovers. It can be mowed several times to produce continued forage. It needs more water than winter annual clovers like subterranean clover. Seed at 9 to 12 pounds per acre (10.1 to 13.4 kg/ha).

Annual Grasses (Tilled in)

- **Ryegrass (*Lolium multiflorum*), cereal oat (*Avena sativa*), and barley (*Hordeum vulgare*).** These produce a large biomass. Start in October to November and irrigate. Till prior to seed maturity. They can also be mowed and placed in the tree row for weed control. They require the addition of nitrogen for a good stand. Seed ryegrass at 10 to 20 pounds per acre (11.2 to 22.4 kg/ha), or if erosion control is necessary, seed at 50 to 60 pounds per acre (56 to 67.2 kg/ha). Seed cereal oat or barley at 60 to 90 pounds per acre (67 to 100.8 kg/ha).

Annual Legumes (Tilled in)

- **Bell bean or fava bean** *(Vicia faba).* Seed this tall-growing (to 6 feet, or 1.8 m) erect vetch annually by November 1 to get good growth prior to cold weather. It can fix 100 pounds (45 kg) of nitrogen in low-nitrogen soils. Seed at 80 to 100 pounds per acre (89.6 to 112 kg/ha).

- **Lana woolypod vetch** *(Vicia villosa* **ssp.** *dasycarpa).* This prolific nitrogen fixer (up to 250 lb/acre, or 280 kg/ha) is seeded in the fall and tilled in the spring. The amount of growth depends on seeding date, winter temperatures, rainfall, and tillage date. It grows well in cold weather: best choice if seeded late. Seed at 15 to 30 pounds per acre (16.8 to 33.6 kg/ha).

- **Common vetch** *(Vicia sativa)* **and purple vetch** *(Vicia benghalensis).* Very similar in growth habits, these two vetches grow well during the winter when seeded in early fall. They will tolerate temperatures of 20°F (–6.7°C) without injury. Seed at 40 to 50 pounds per acre (44.8 to 56 kg/ha).

- **Hairy vetch** *(Vicia villosa).* This vetch is better adapted to sandy soils. It is also very cold tolerant but does not grow much during the winter. Seed at 40 to 50 pounds per acre (44.8 to 56 kg/ha).

- **Field pea (Austrian winter pea)** *(Pisum sativum).* This grows like garden pea. It remains almost dormant in cold weather, but growth surges in the spring. Seed at 70 to 90 pounds per acre (78.4 to 100.8 kg/ha).

- **Fenugreek** *(Trigonella foenum-graecum).* Fenugreek germinates in cold conditions as late as December and provides a good stand. Seed at 40 to 50 pounds per acre (44.8 to 56 kg/ha).

ACKNOWLEDGMENT

The authors acknowledge the contribution of Dr. Roland D. Meyer, Soil and Water Specialist, University of California, Davis.

REFERENCES

Barranco, D., R. Fernández-Escobar, and L. Rallo. 2001. El Cultivo del olivo. 4th ed. Madrid: Ediciones Mundi-Prensa.

Beutel, J., K. Uriu, and O. Lilleland. 1983. Leaf analysis for California deciduous fruits. In H. M. Reisenauer, ed., Soil and plant tissue testing in California. Oakland: University of California Division of Agriculture and Natural Resources Bulletin 1879.

Connell, J. H., and P. Catlin. 2005. Root physiology and rootstock characteristics. In G. S. Sibbett and L. Ferguson, eds., Olive production manual. 2nd ed. Oakland: University of California Division of Agriculture and Natural Resources Publication 3353. 39–47.

Freeman, M., and R. M. Carlson. 2005. Mineral nutrition availability. In G. S. Sibbett and L. Ferguson, eds., Olive production manual. 2nd ed. Oakland: University of California Division of Agriculture and Natural Resources Publication 3353. 75–82.

Freeman, M., K. Uriu, and H. T. Hartman. 2005. Diagnosing and correcting nutrient problems. In G. S. Sibbett and L. Ferguson, eds., Olive production manual. 2nd ed. Oakland: University of California Division of Agriculture and Natural Resources Publication 3353. 83–92.

Gonzálvez V., and R. Muñoz. 2002. La Olivicultura ecológica en españa. Ubeda, Spain: Editora y Distribuidora El Olivo.

O'Malley, K., J. Bentivoglio, C. Beckingham, and D. Conlan. 2003. Organic olive management: A guide for Australian olive growers. Pendle Hill: New South Wales Agriculture and Australian Olive Association.

Pastor, M., and J. Castro. 1995. Soil management systems and erosion. Olivae Magazine 59 (Dec.): 64–74.

Swezey, S., P. Vossen, J. Caprile, and W. Bentley, eds. 1999. Organic apple production manual. Oakland: University of California Division of Agriculture and Natural Resources Publication 3403.

Vossen, P. M. 2003. Fertilizing olive trees: Nutrition is less important than water. Olea 6(1): 4–5.

Part 3
Pest Management in Organic Olive Production

6

Monitoring and Organic Control of Olive Fruit Fly

ALEXANDRA KICENIK DEVARENNE AND PAUL M. VOSSEN

INTRODUCTION

The most economically significant pest of olives is the olive fruit fly (*Bactrocera (Dacus) oleae*) (plate 6.1). It was probably introduced into California from the Mediterranean region, where there are records of infestations dating back to the third century BC. It is also found in North Africa and the Middle East. The olive fly occurs along the coast of eastern and southern Africa and in South Africa, where there are relatively few commercial olive plantings but wild olive trees are found.

The olive fruit fly was identified for the first time in the United States on October 19, 1998, in West Los Angeles. The fly was caught in a McPhail trap in a lemon tree, part of a Mexican fruit fly detection program. After this initial discovery, it was detected in coastal California from Santa Barbara County to San Diego County and inland to Riverside and San Bernardino Counties. By early 2000, detection trapping was abandoned in Ventura and Santa Barbara Counties because of the general infestation. The fly has advanced northward in California and now infests all the major olive-producing areas of the state.

ECONOMIC IMPORTANCE AND DAMAGE

The olive fruit fly belongs to the family Tephritidae, a group that includes such economically important flies as the Mediterranean fruit fly (*Ceratitis capitata*), the walnut husk fly (*Rhagoletis completa*), the apple maggot (*R. pomonella*), and the Oriental fruit fly (*Bactrocera dorsalis*). The adult female can lay 50 to 400 eggs in her lifetime, usually one in each fruit. These hatch into tiny larvae (maggots) that are very difficult to see until they feed for a while and get larger. While feeding, they tunnel throughout the fruit, destroying the pulp and allowing secondary infestations of bacteria and fungi that rot the fruit. This damage greatly increases the free fatty acid level (acidity) of the olive oil and causes off-flavors. Feeding damage may also cause premature fruit drop. Oviposition stings, caused by the female laying eggs inside the olive, destroy the value of table fruit even if larval damage is not present.

DESCRIPTION

The adult fly (see plate 6.1) is usually about 3/16 inch long (4 to 5 mm) and reddish brown in color, with large eyes and small antennae. The top of the thorax (trunk) is dark brown with gray or black longitudinal stripes and a white crescent-shaped spot (scutellum) located to the rear of where the wings are attached. There are also several yellow-white patches on each side of the thorax. The abdomen is brown with darker variable areas on the sides of each segment. The wings are clear with a small dark spot near the tip and can be distinguished from those of other Tephritid fruit flies that have dark wing bands or patterns. The females have a point at the tip of the abdomen (ovipositor). The sheath of the ovipositor is black and the ovipositor is reddish. The larvae are yellowish white legless maggots with a point on one end (the head) (plate 6.2).

LIFE CYCLE AND BIOLOGY

The olive fruit fly has three to five generations per year, depending on local conditions. It overwinters either as an adult or as a pupa in the soil or fallen fruit. Overwintered adult populations decline to low levels by February or March, but under ideal conditions adult flies can live for over 6 months. In mild climates adults can emerge continuously throughout the year, but larger numbers of new adults from over-wintered pupae begin to emerge in March and April. These females can lay eggs inside last year's fruit left on the tree or wait until new fruit is large enough for oviposition. The ability of the fruit to sustain larval development begins around the time of pit harden-ing. High populations can develop very rapidly when ideal temperature favors rapid development. In most cases, the greatest damage occurs from September to November.

The second generation appears in midsummer. The olive fly can complete a generation in as little as 30 to 35 days at optimal temperatures from 68° to 86°F (20° to 30°C). Eggs hatch in 2 to 3 days; larvae develop in approximately 20 days, and pupae in 8 to 10 days. During the winter, the pupal phase can last 6 months. The maggots feed throughout the olive and pupate in a hollow area just beneath the outer skin, or they can exit the fruit and pupate in the soil. Adult flies can live from 2 to 7 months depending on the temperature and availability of food (honeydew, fruit juices, bird feces, etc.). Additional generations of flies are produced through the late summer and fall months into December, depending on fruit availability. Olives left on trees after harvest can produce high popula-tions of flies from late fall to early spring. Most of the last-generation larvae abandon the fruit to pupate in the ground for several months. Adults can overwinter in protected areas, especially in locations with mild winter temperatures.

Plants in the genus *Olea* are the only breeding host plants for this fly. The larger cultivars of *Olea europea* are preferred for oviposition; however, smaller oil olive varieties are also susceptible. The flies can also breed in wild olives. Flies have been trapped in other crop orchards and landscape plants, including citrus, plum, apple, chestnut, fig, arbutus, and sycamore, where the adults search for food or refuge.

Olive flies survive best in cooler coastal climates, but they are also found in hot, dry regions of Greece, Italy, Spain, Mexico, and California. Temperatures above 95°F (35°C) are detrimental to adult flies and to maggots in the fruit. The flies, however, can travel to seek out cooler areas where water is available. Reports of fly movement range from 600 feet (183 m) in the presence of an olive host to several miles. The olive fruit fly spread throughout California at a rate of about 100 miles (160 km) per year, indicating great mobil-ity. During rainy winter weather the number of flies caught in traps usually drops off significantly, but stings and damage can continue.

DAMAGE THRESHOLDS

In Europe, the damage threshold for commercial table fruit orchards is 10 percent, but California table fruit processors have zero tolerance for olive fruit fly dam-age. The backyard table olive producer may be willing to accept higher levels of olive fly damage since the damaged fruit can be sorted out by hand.

Oviposition stings show up as small brown spots on the olive. To confirm that a spot is a viable olive fly sting, shave slices off the olive where the brown speck appears. The presence of a thin brown line in the flesh of the olive indicates that a larva has begun tunneling. Advanced olive fly damage appears as blackened areas on otherwise green fruit, dimpling and distortion in the shape of the olive, and finally as a light brown exit hole about 1/12 inch (2 mm) in diameter (plate 6.3). If you cut into a fruit with advanced damage you will find large tunnels and an obvious larva or pupa.

The most commonly cited European damage threshold level for olive oil production is 10 percent. However, research has shown that even with 100 per-cent of the fruit sustaining olive fly damage, acceptable olive oil can be produced as long as the fruit shows no signs of rot. Oil from fly-damaged olives does not keep well, however, developing pronounced defective flavors over time. There is an immediate oil quality problem when larval feeding introduces fruit-rotting organisms that create off-flavors. Since this is more likely to happen toward the end of the larval feeding cycle when the maggots are larger, earlier harvest may be one of the options for dealing with this pest. It is also important to note that when olives are damaged by olive fruit fly, the fruit is more sensitive to oxidative and microbial breakdown. Therefore, the time from harvest to milling should be kept as short as possible. Research is being conducted in California to establish specific damage threshold levels. At the present, each olive oil mill has its own guidelines, and producers should consult their miller regarding acceptable dam-age levels.

SANITATION

To reduce or prevent olive fly, start with sanitation. Any olives that remain on the tree or the ground at the end of the season should be removed and either buried or sealed in a bag for landfill disposal. In situations where discing an orchard is practical, it may reduce the size of the spring generation by burying overwintering pupae too deep for emergence, at least 12 inches (31 cm). If last season's olives remain on the tree, they may provide a site for oviposition by olive flies in the spring.

TRAPPING FOR MONITORING AND CONTROL

Using traps to check for the presence and activity of olive flies can be a useful part of a control program, but caution should be used in interpreting the trap catches. Low trap catches do not necessarily correlate with low damage levels. If olive fly is present, it is prudent to inspect fruit frequently for stings and to initiate a control program. Yellow sticky traps are currently the monitoring standard in California, but McPhail trap catches tend to be higher and may be a better indicator of the fly population. Use at least two traps per orchard block for monitoring. Traps should be checked weekly and the olive flies removed to avoid confusion when keeping the weekly tally.

Mass trapping is the use of traps for control. For mass trapping, traps are placed at a high density, up to one trap per tree. A few traps may be monitored weekly, but the majority of the traps are just maintained in an effective condition. During recent field trials, when yellow sticky, McPhail, and OLIPE traps were used at the rate of one per tree in small plantings at various different sites, the damage levels averaged around 30 percent compared to 87 percent in our untreated controls (Vossen and Devarenne 2006). The "Attract and Kill" device averaged about 15 percent damage. Although mass trapping may not provide adequate control as a stand-alone measure, the reduction in the fly population may improve the efficacy of bait sprays and allow for less-frequent application.

The success of area-wide mass trapping for fruit flies in Hawaii is encouraging. Research is continuing in California to determine whether a mass trapping campaign can be made more effective by covering a larger area.

Yellow Sticky Panel Trap

Yellow sticky traps baited with a sex lure (spiroketal pheromone) and a food attractant (ammonium carbonate or ammonium bicarbonate) are used to capture both male and female adult flies. The bait packet and pheromone lure hang on the top edge of the trap (plate 6.4).

Hang the trap in the shade on the north side of a tree with fruit, inside the canopy, with 8 to 10 inches (21 to 26 cm) of clearance from foliage. Traps can last from 1 to 8 weeks depending on how dirty they get (and thus how sticky they remain). Change the bait packets and lures according to the manufacturer's recommendations. Although most commonly used for monitoring, yellow sticky traps can also be used for mass trapping. They are fast and easy to hang, but do require maintenance to assure that the surface remains sticky. Dust and insects can quickly make a yellow panel trap ineffective. Disposable gloves are helpful for protecting your hands from the sticky coating when handling the traps.

McPhail Trap

The McPhail trap is used extensively for monitoring and for mass trapping. Traditionally, the McPhail trap is made of glass, but plastic types are becoming the norm (plate 6.5).

All McPhail traps have a reservoir for liquid bait and a large opening at the bottom of the trap. In California, torula yeast is the most prevalent bait attractant, but in Europe various ammonium solutions are used as well. Flies enter from below and drown in the solution. McPhail traps tend to have the highest catches of all the common traps. They also require the most maintenance because of their tendency to dry out in hot weather. Ten percent propylene glycol may be added to the liquid bait mixture to reduce evaporation and better preserve the flies. McPhail traps must be hung in the shade, and the water level must be checked frequently. Use three torula yeast bait tablets per trap and add water to the fill line. Change the solution at least once per month. In a comparison between red and yellow McPhail traps, the yellow outperformed the red consistently (Vossen and Devarenne 2006). There was also no difference in trap catches when pheromone lures were added to the traps.

OLIPE

A low-cost trap called the OLIPE (Olivarera los Pedroches) trap was developed in Spain for organic ("Ecological") production. It consists of a 1- to 2-liter (1.1- to 2.1-qt) plastic nonfood bottle with 5-millimeter (3/16-inch) holes drilled or melted around the shoulder (plate 6.6).

In Spain the attractant used is a 3 to 5 percent solution of ammonium bicarbonate, ammonium carbonate, or diammonium phosphate. Field trials in California comparing different baits in the OLIPE found that a solution of torula yeast caught four times as many olive flies as the ammonium solutions (Vossen 2005). In Spain a pheromone is added when the fly pressure is high, but trials in California using various spiroketal pheromone and combination lures have failed to show any advantage. Use three torula yeast tablets to about 1 liter of water as an attractant and hang the bottle in the shade. The OLIPE requires much less maintenance than the McPhail because it does not dry out as quickly, but the yeast solution should still be changed periodically.

Attract and Kill Device

The "Attract and kill" olive fly target device is used in Europe for olive fly control. There it is called the Eco-trap, and it is especially popular for organic production. It consists of a shallow lambda cyhalothrin–impregnated cardboard cone with a bait and/or sex lure (plate 6.7).

The fly is attracted by the lures, encounters the pesticide in the cardboard, and dies. The pesticide does not come in contact with the fruit or the environment. The trap lasts the entire season and requires no maintenance, making it very convenient. In field trials in small orchards and backyard trees, the trap was placed at a density of one per tree, but in a larger orchard the recommended density is from 40 to 60 traps per acre (99 to 148 per ha) (Vossen 2005). The trap is manufactured in the United Kingdom and will be sold in the United States under the name Magnet OL. The Magnet OL target device has not been approved in the United States for certified organic production.

Bait Spray

GF-120 Naturalyte is a bait spray containing the active ingredient spinosad. Spinosad is a fermentation by-product of the actinomycete bacteria *Saccharopolyspora spinosa*.

The bait is a formulation of hydrolyzed protein. The U.S. Department of Agriculture (USDA) Organic Materials Review Institute (OMRI) standards board has approved spinosad for certified organic production.

GF-120 is diluted and applied in a coarse spray or stream to a small portion of the tree (plate 6.8). There is no need to cover the whole tree; the adult flies are attracted to the bait, feed on it, and die. The treated area should stay wet as long as possible, so applying it very early in the morning or very late in the afternoon is best. One or two sprays in the late winter or early spring as soon as fly catches in monitor traps show an increase may help to reduce the population. In order to achieve adequate control in heavily infested orchards, most growers apply the material every week from late spring to harvest. Light infestations may be treated with applications every two weeks.

GF-120 provided very good control in recent trials, with damage levels averaging around 3 percent compared with untreated controls, which suffered 87 percent damage. When GF-120 was applied after 20 percent fly damage was apparent, the damage was effectively stopped at that percentage. Subsequent damage assessments showed very little new damage, although the larvae that were already present continued to mature and emerge. GF-120 appears to be relatively safe for beneficial insects. The bait is not particularly attractive to honey bees, and since it must be consumed to be effective, it has a low impact. It also seems to have little toxicity for lady beetles. The effect of GF-120 on parasitic wasps and lacewings is an area of concern and further research is needed (Michaud 2003).

Barrier Spray

Kaolin clay (brand name Surround) is a particle film that is also approved for certified organic production. The product is mixed with water and applied with a high-pressure sprayer in order to get good coverage. The solution dries to a white powder, which repels the olive flies (plate 6.9). The exact mechanism by which the film repels the flies is not known. Kaolin clay has no known nutrient value for plants, nor is it toxic to insects; the mode of action is thought to be tactile or visual in nature. The first application should be a week or two before pit hardening, and it should be reapplied every 5 or 6 weeks. The control in our trials with Surround was comparable to GF-120, averaging around 3 percent damage. We also noted that the olives treated with Surround were larger than the olives on neighboring trees.

REFERENCES

CDFA (California Department of Food and Agriculture) Olive Fruit Fly Pest Profile Web site, http://www.cdfa.ca.gov/phpps/pdep/olive_ff_profile.htm.

Civantos López-Villalta, M. 1999. Olive pest and disease management. International Olive Oil Council. Madrid, Spain.

Michaud, J. P. 2003. Toxicity of fruit fly baits to beneficial insects in citrus. Journal of Insect Science (Mar.).

Rice, R. 2000. Bionomics of the olive fruit fly, *Bactrocera (Dacus) oleae*. UC Plant Protection Quarterly 10:3.

University of California Cooperative Extension Sonoma County Web site, http://cesonoma.ucdavis.edu/hortic/research pubs.html.

Van Steenwyk, R. A., L. Ferguson, and F. G. Zalom. 2004. UC pest management guidelines: Olives. Oakland: University of California Agriculture and Natural Resources Publication 3452. University of California Integrated Pest Management Web site, http://www.ipm.ucdavis.edu/PMG/r583301311.html.

Vossen, P. M. 2005. Organic control measures for olive fruit fly in small-scale orchards and landscapes in Coastal California. Symposium: IPM in organic production systems. Pacific Branch Entomological Society of America 8th Annual Meeting, Asilomar, CA. Feb. 27–Mar. 2.

Vossen, P. M., and A. Devarenne. n.d. Controlling olive fruit fly at home. University of California Cooperative Extension Sonoma County Web site, http://cesonoma.ucdavis.edu/hortic/pdf/olive_fruit_fly_home.pdf.

———. 2006. Comparison of mass trapping, barrier film, and spinosad bait for the control of olive fruit fly in small-scale orchards and landscapes in coastal California. Proceedings of the 8th Exotic Fruit Fly Symposium. Riverside: University of California, Riverside, College of Agricultural and Natural Sciences.

Zalom, F. G., R. A. Van Steenwyk, and H. J. Burrack. UC IPM olive fruit fly pest note. 2003. Oakland: University of California Agriculture and Natural Resources Publication 74112. University of California Integrated Pest Management Web site, http://www.ipm.ucdavis.edu/PMG/PESTNOTES/pn74112.html.

7

Organic Management of Common Insects and Diseases of Olive

WILLIAM H. KRUEGER AND PAUL M. VOSSEN

INTRODUCTION

Fortunately, olives have very few pest problems that require protective synthetic chemicals, and in almost all cases, alternative organic materials or procedures can be used. Often, control measures are the same for organic and conventional production. In some cases, organic insect and disease control options may be less effective, more costly, and thereby subject the grower to greater risk than conventional methods.

OLIVE KNOT

Comments on the Disease

Olive knot is caused by the bacterium *Pseudomonas syringae* pv. *savastanoi*. The disease is spread by wind and rain and gains entry into the tree through openings such as leaf scars (most common), pruning wounds, frost cracks, and hail damage. Infection occurs in the fall, winter, and spring and gives rise to rough galls or swellings of disorganized tissue 1/2 to 2 inches (1.2 to 2.5 cm) in diameter on twigs, branches, trunks, roots, leaves, or fruit stems when tree growth resumes in the spring (plate 7.1). Smaller branches usually become girdled and die. This disease does not kill the tree, but can greatly reduce its productivity. It can be very severe following freezes or hail damage that results in defoliation, frost cracks, or ruptured bark during a time when rainfall is imminent. Bacteria survive in the knots and are spread by water at all times of the year. The period of heaviest infection is during the spring, coinciding with natural leaf drop (Teviotdale and Krueger 2004). No cultivars are immune, but they differ in susceptibility (table 7.1).

Table 7.1. Olive variety susceptibility to three important diseases

Variety	Peacock spot *Spilocaea oleaginae*	Verticillium wilt *Verticillium dahliae*	Olive knot *Pseudomonas syringae* pv. *savastanoi*
Aglandau	S	R	—
Arbequina	S	VS	VS
Arbosana	VR	—	—
Ascolano	S	R	R
Blanqueta	VS	—	R
Bouteillan	R	—	—
Cayon	R	—	—
Coratina	R	—	—
Cornicabra	VS	VS	—
Empeltre	VS	VR	S
Frantoio	VR	VR	R
Gordal Sevillana	S	S	S
Hojiblanca	S	VS	S
Kalamon	S	S	R
Koroneiki	VR	R	S
Leccino	R	S	R
Manzanilla	S	S	VS
Maurino	R	—	—
Mission	VS	S	R
Moraiolo	R	S	S
P. Marocaine	VS	—	R
Pendolino	S	S	S
Picholine	S	S	—
Picual	VS	VS	S
Picudo	S	VS	VS

Source: Blanco-López and López-Escudero 2005; Peñalver et al. 2005; Trapero and López-Doncel 2005.

Key: VR = very resistant; R = resistant; S = susceptible; VS = very susceptible.

Disease severity is generally positively correlated with annual rainfall (Krueger et al. 1999). It is interesting to note, however, that olive knot is almost completely absent from coastal areas of California.

Management

There is no effective curative treatment for olive knot. Control is preventative. Where possible, plant more-resistant varieties in areas of high rainfall or where disease pressure is known to be high. Avoid making openings for the disease by injuring the tree during rainy periods. Delay pruning until the risk of freeze injury has passed and the likelihood of rain is reduced. Pruning wounds remain susceptible to infection for approximately 2 weeks during cool, wet periods (Krueger et al. 1999) (less time under dry, warm conditions). Pruning in the fall or winter opens tree canopies and makes the trees more susceptible to freeze damage resulting in leaf scars and frost cracks, which can become infected. Reduce the disease inoculum by pruning out as much infected wood as feasible during the pruning operation.

Copper sprays protect infection sites, but they must be applied before the infection occurs. Copper residues are redistributed with rainfall and provide some protection to openings that occur after application. Multiple sprays are recommended in areas of high disease pressure or during wet years (Teviotdale and Krueger 2004). Generally, a postharvest spray followed by a spring spray (March or April) is recommended. A spray should be applied immediately following events that injure the tree and make openings, such as freeze or hail damage.

If the orchard is nonbearing, it can be sprayed any-time, but, because copper residues are hard to remove, bearing trees should not be sprayed near harvest. Organically acceptable formulations of copper include Bordeaux spray (copper sulfate and hydrated lime) and various fixed coppers, such as copper oxide.

The national list of acceptable products for use in organic production changes from time to time. New products are added and some products are removed or allowed only for restricted purposes. Always consult the current national list of allowed and prohibited substances, and never use any substance without your certification agent's written approval.

PEACOCK SPOT AND CERCOSPORA LEAF SPOT

Comments on the Disease

Two fungal foliar diseases of olive must be managed in order to have highly productive orchards. The most common is peacock spot, caused by *Spilocaea oleaginea*. This fungus disease causes dark, circular spots $1/16$ to $1/2$ inch (1.5 to 12 mm) in diameter on the leaves with a yellow halo developing later around each spot (plate 7.2). Eventually the rest of the leaf yellows and drops.

Cercospora leaf spot, the other defoliating disease, is caused by the fungus *Mycocentrospora cladosporioides*, which has been isolated from orchards on the north coast of California. Cercospora leaf spot causes sooty-mold-like symptoms (from the conidia) on the underside of the leaves, yellowing, and leaf drop without leaf spots.

These two diseases develop under very similar conditions. The resulting premature leaf drop weakens the trees and reduces crop set. Inoculum levels for peacock spot and probably Cercospora leaf spot can build in orchards and have a carry-over effect from year to year (Teviotdale et al. 1989). Infection occurs during rainy periods, but symptoms do not become apparent until growth commences in the spring, sometimes several months after infection. Disease development is positively correlated with rainfall. Infection can occur in temperatures from 35° to 80°F (1.7° to 26.7°C), but the optimal temperature is 58° to 75°F (14.4 to 23.9°C). About 48 hours of free moisture is necessary for spores to infect the leaves. During dry winters, infection is minimal. Both old and young leaves are vulnerable to infection. Most varieties are susceptible, but susceptibility is variable (see table 7.1). Peacock spot and Cercospora are much worse in low-lying areas or under conditions of heavy dew, fog, high humidity, low sunlight, closed tree canopies, or excessive sprinkler irrigation.

Management

Control of these diseases requires a preventive strategy. Both diseases are more severe in areas of high rainfall or late-spring or summer rains. The diseases may even limit where olives can be successfully grown. In areas where these diseases are prevalent, try to avoid growing the most susceptible cultivars (see table 7.1). For susceptible varieties, the only reliable control is covering the leaves with protectant copper fungicide sprays (the same materials used for controlling olive knot). Copper treatments should be applied before major fall and winter rains have a chance to spread the spores to the new leaves, but they should not be applied to the fruit prior to harvest. It is uncertain, but highly likely, that an additional spring application in wet years would be beneficial. Complete coverage of the foliage is necessary. These two foliar diseases are not significantly affected by tree nutrition, but excessive nitrogen and low calcium may predispose the trees to greater infection. Foliar nutrients and compost tea sprays have not proven to be effective. A consistent spray program to prevent the buildup of inoculum is recommended.

....

VERTICILLIUM WILT

Comments on the Disease

Verticillium wilt, caused by the fungus *Verticillium dahliae*, is a serious disease in olives (and many other crops as well) for which there is no cure. The pathogen is a soil-inhabiting fungus that attacks roots and grows into the vascular tissue of the tree, plugging the tissue and causing sudden wilting and the death of limbs and entire trees. Verticillium wilt can be a limiting factor for economic olive production in areas with high incidence of infection such as the southern San Joaquin Valley. Inoculum levels can build up in locations where host plants such as cotton, tomato, potato, pepper, eggplant, or squash have been grown, or in areas with a prevalence of nightshade family weeds. The fungus can persist in the soil for several years as microsclerotia, small multicelled structures that remain quiescent until stimulated by the proximity of root growth of a suitable host.

The primary symptom of Verticillium wilt is a sudden browning of the leaves on a single branch; the leaves stick to the dead branch, unlike the symptoms of Armillaria root rot (see below), in which defoliation appears gradually and the leaves drop out of the canopy (plate 7.3). Symptoms often appear with the onset of summer heat. Unlike many other susceptible plants, darkening of xylem tissues is not readily apparent in olive, so for positive identification, a branch sample that has both dead and live tissue must be sent to a plant pathology laboratory. Entire orchards have been killed by this disease when trees were planted in heavily infested soil. Of the several strains of the fungus, the most virulent is the cotton defoliating strain, named for its symptoms on cotton.

Management

The most effective steps to protect olive trees from Verticillium wilt must be taken before planting. Choose a planting site that has not been planted for a number of years to crops that are highly susceptible to Verticillium wilt, such as cotton. The presence or absence of microsclerotia in soil samples is the criteria used to identify the potential hazard. There is no known quantitative rating system based on microsclerotia numbers. The amount of inoculum can be reduced by soil solarization, flooding, or growing cover crops such as sudangrass (*Sorghum bicolor*) or corn that will not support the fungus for at least 2 years. Solarization is done by covering the entire weed-free, moist surface area with clear plastic throughout the summer. Steps should be taken to prevent the introduction of *Verticillium* onto the farm. Make sure no soil or infested plant debris is brought onto the farm from trucks or farm equipment. Limit water movement from infested soils into noninfested sites. Do not intercrop olives with susceptible plant hosts. Avoid tree manipulations that cause excessive vegetative growth such as applying excessive nitrogen fertilizers or heavy pruning. Broadleaf nightshade family weeds that harbor *Verticillium*, including nightshade and horsenettle (*Solanum* spp.), groundcherry (*Physalis* spp.), thornapple (*Datura* spp.), and henbane (*Hyoscyamus* spp.), should not be allowed to grow in the orchard. No known rootstocks have successfully protected trees from this disease.

....

ARMILLARIA ROOT ROT (OAK ROOT FUNGUS)

Comments on the Disease

The causal agent of Armillaria root rot is a fungus (*Armillaria mellea*) that attacks numerous tree species, but the disease is rarely observed in olives. It usually occurs in orchards where oak trees were native and is worse following wet winters or where very wet areas form around the crowns of the trees from sprinkler irrigation. It is sometimes confused with Verticillium wilt because the initial symptoms are similar in that one branch on a tree often wilts and dies first before the disease progresses to kill the whole tree. With Armillaria root rot, however, the affected branches look weak and retain a few leaves and the branches die more slowly than with Verticillium wilt. It usually affects one tree in an orchard and may spread to adjacent trees, probably through root-to-root transmission. To confirm the disease, dig around the base of the tree and expose the crown area, especially on the side with the affected branch, and remove some of the bark. The area under the bark will appear white with fan-shaped mycelial growth (plaques) (plate 7.4), and black stringlike structures (rhizomorphs) may be evident. The bark will smell like fresh mushrooms. In the winter you may see mushrooms, the fruiting body of the fungi, attached to the tree trunks. A sample taken from this area and sent to a plant pathology lab can positively identify the disease.

Management

If possible, avoid planting in areas where oak trees have recently been removed or in areas with a history of Armillaria root rot. Once a tree is infected, it likely cannot be saved, but drying out the area immediately adjacent to the tree may prolong the life of the tree. The best thing to do is to remove the infected tree and as many of the roots as possible with a backhoe, then treat the soil with solarization as described for Verticillium wilt, above. There are no known Armillaria-resistant rootstocks for olive. Soil solarization is only moderately effective, but it is the only alternative for organic growers.

PHYTOPHTHORA CROWN AND ROOT ROT

Comments on the Disease

Root and crown rot is not a common problem in olive trees, but it can kill or weaken trees in excessively wet or poorly drained soils. The disease is caused by any of several species of *Phytophthora*, a soilborne funguslike organism. To date, *P. citricola* and two unidentified species have been isolated from symptomatic trees (Teviotdale 2005). *Phytophthora drechleri* has been shown to be highly virulent on olives in greenhouse studies.

Saturated soil conditions are necessary for infection. Olive trees do not tolerate excessively wet soils. Poor aeration in the soil can cause many of the symptoms described below, but symptoms and tree death develop more rapidly and can be more severe when Phytophthora is involved. The first symptoms usually occur in the spring in low-lying areas or areas with heavier soil, but affected trees can also be randomly located in an orchard. Trees appear weak with little new growth, yellowing leaves, and thinning canopies. Large branches and entire trees may die. In order to identify the disease, uncover the lower part of the crown and the upper part of the root system. Remove some bark in the area. Infected tissue will be dark brown or black (plate 7.5).

Management

Phytophthora crown and root rot can be prevented by not planting olives in areas with poor drainage. Sites that have poor surface drainage that cannot be corrected or very heavy clay soils (poor internal drainage) are not appropriate for most olive orchards. Planting trees on berms or ridges so that the crown of the tree dries rapidly after rain or irrigation is advisable where soils or conditions may be conducive to the disease. Manage irrigation to avoid saturated soil conditions for more than 24 hours. Avoid tree stress during the growing season and keep irrigation water away from the area immediately adjacent to the tree trunks. No fungicide treatments are known to be effective.

BLACK SCALE (SOFT SCALE)

Description of the Pest

Black scale (*Saissetia oleae*) is a soft scale insect that is a very common pest of olives. The adult females look like black convex shells about 3/16 inch (5 mm) in diameter, with a ridged H on the back (plate 7.6).

Heavy infestations can stunt plant growth and reduce flowering and fruiting. The heaviest feeding occurs in the spring and autumn (April and October). Scales attach themselves to leaves and small shoots and suck the sap, secreting honeydew that drips and sticks on plant surfaces and the ground. A sooty mold fungus grows on the honeydew, leaving a black, dusty, sticky residue that reduces photosynthesis and respiration. The combination of insect feeding and sooty mold can reduce fruit bud development, cause defoliation and twig dieback, and reduce the crop the following year (Sibbett et al. 1976). Black scale prefers cool coastal climates and survives better in dense, shady portions of the trees. It can develop to injurious levels in warmer climates such as the Central Valley during cool summers or in trees with dense canopies. It may have one to two generations per year (usually just one in hot areas). The brown adults change to black as they mature and have a distinct hemispherical shape. Eggs develop under the adult female's soft shell. After hatching, the tiny crawlers (first-instar nymphs) move out over new tissue and settle down to feed at different times of the growing season, depending on the local climate. The crawler stage is pale yellow to light brown, a fraction the size of adults, and is the stage most susceptible to control. The second-instar nymphs develop 3 to 8 weeks after hatching and have a distinctive H-shaped pattern beginning to develop on the back. They are intermediate in susceptibility to control. The third instars are almost the size of adults and are dark brown to ashy gray, with a distinctive H-shaped pattern on the back.

Management

Many natural enemies have been imported and released to control black scale. About 15 parasitoid wasp species have become established (Daane et al. 2005). Of these, three *Metaphycus* species, two *Coccophagus* species, and one *Scutillista* species are the most common. *Metaphycus helvolus*, probably the most important, is commercially available. Insect predators are also present, such as lacewings (*Chrysoperla* spp.) and lady beetles such as *Hippodamia convergens* and *Hyperaspis* spp. Unfortunately, parasitoids and predators have been only partially successful at controlling black scale levels below economic thresholds, especially in warmer climates. The limited number of host generations per year limits suitable host stages for the parasitoids. *Metaphycus* should be released when the young scales begin to develop the H-shaped ridges. Ants can be disruptive to biological control. They feed on the honeydew produced by soft scales and protect them from parasitoids and predators. Controlling ants may enhance biological control. They can be kept out of the trees by applying Tanglefoot to the tree trunks and pruning up the skirts or placing organically acceptable ant bait at the base of infested trees. Liquid sugar baits containing organically acceptable boric acid will be available in 2007 or 2008 and can be placed in EPA-approved bait stations (Grafton-Cardwell and Godfrey 2005).

Biological control is more reliable and effective in cooler climates. In warmer climates, steps taken to enhance heat mortality, such as pruning to create open, airy canopies, will usually provide adequate control. Black scale populations can build during cool springs and summers and may not be noticed until harvest.

If the above methods do not provide adequate control, a spray treatment may be necessary. The only organically certified spray treatment material is narrow range oil (summer oil or superior oil) (Flint et al. 2004). It is not phytotoxic to the leaves as long as the temperature is not too high, over 90°F (32.2°C). Oils should be sprayed at night or when temperatures will be cool for a few days. Treatments should be applied at the crawler stage after the eggs have hatched. Monitor adult scales and treat after the eggs have hatched, usually during July to mid-August in the Central Valley. Crawler emergence can be monitored by wrapping double-sided sticky tape around small limbs in areas with scale infestation. When the crawlers emerge they will be caught in the tape. All crawlers have emerged when no unhatched eggs can be seen under the adult females. Treatments applied after August 1 may be too late to avoid a reduction in flowering and fruit set the following year (Sibbett et al. 1976).

Monitor black scale by checking trees in the spring and fall, especially in areas where black scale has been seen in the past. Sample the terminal 18 inches (45 cm) on ten branches on ten different trees. Count the number of adults on each tree making sure to include branches from the lower and inner portions of the trees. Look for evidence of parasitism (exit holes in the scale made by parasitoids). Sum the numbers on each ten-branch sample and divide by the number of branches. Light infestations have less than 1 scale per branch, medium infestations have 1 to 4 per branch, heavy infestations have from 4 to 10 per branch, and severe infestations have more than 10 scale insects per branch. Light to medium infestations can usually be controlled by pruning trees and controlling the ants. Medium (if the weather is favorable) or worse infestations will usually need to be sprayed. Treatments should be applied to get thorough coverage of the upper and lower surface of leaves, which usually requires 300 to 500 gallons per acre (28.1 to 26.8 hl/ha) of applied material on large trees.

....

OLEANDER SCALE AND OLIVE SCALE

Description of the Pest

These two armored scales differ from soft scales like black scale in that they have waxy coverings that are not part of the insect. These scales are much smaller than black scale, 1/16 to 1/8 inch (1.5 to 3 mm) in diameter, and are flattened and look like small encrustations on the leaves or shoots (plates 7.7 and 7.8).

Oleander scale and olive scale are similar but differ slightly from one another in their color, effect on the olive fruit, number of generations per year, and timing of the crawler stage. Light infestations do not pose a significant threat, but heavy infestations can reduce productivity and increase the amount of off-grade product in table olives due to distorted fruit growth and uneven maturation of fruit tissue.

Oleander scale (*Aspidiotus nerii*) (see plate 7.7) has a waxy shell covering that is almost white with a yellow or brown spot near its center. The scale body is yellow underneath the waxy covering. Oleander scale may have several generations per year that can deform the fruit and significantly reduce oil production. As fruit ripens and begins to color, a small area of the fruit around the scale remains green. Olive scale, also known as Parlatoria scale (*Parlatoria oleae*), has a gray waxy shell and two generations per year. The scale body underneath the waxy covering is purple (see plate 7.9). The spring brood feeds on leaves and branches and deforms fruit. Feeding from the summer generation results in dark purple or black areas around the scales on green fruit before the rest of the fruit turns color.

Management

Prior to 1960, olive scale was a troubling pest that often required treatment to avoid damaging levels of infestation. The introduction of the parasitic wasps *Aphytis maculicornis* and *Coccophagoides utilis* during the 1950s reduced infestations to the point where treatments are seldom necessary. Oleander scale is also usually under good biological control by several species in the *Aphytis* genus and seldom reaches levels that require treatment. Care should be taken to avoid disrupting this biological control.

If troubling levels of any of the armored scales are seen on leaves, shoots, or fruit, the orchard should be monitored more closely to determine the amount of biological control that may be present. Look for small exit holes in the scales' shells that indicate parasite emergence. If this is observed frequently, no further control measures are likely needed. Olive trees should also be pruned to open them up and reduce the amount of dense foliage that favors the scale insects. If, however, the level of damage is heavy, narrow range oil sprays may need to be applied. Biological control and oil sprays are acceptable for organic production.

Before treating with any spray materials, armored scales should be monitored for crawlers by placing double-sided sticky tape on several small branches in the orchard in the spring and checking this tape weekly. This is the best way to determine when the crawlers, the most easily controlled stage, are present. Treating between broods when crawlers are not present is less effective. Postharvest treatments may work well if crawlers are present at that time. For light infestations, treating with oil alone is usually quite effective when combined with pruning to open up the canopy. Heavier infestations may need to be treated in the summer and after harvest. More information on these and other pests and diseases can be found in the *Olive Production Manual* (Sibbett and Ferguson 2005) and the *UC IPM Pest Management Guidelines for Olives* (Van Steenwyk et al. 2004).

REFERENCES

Blanco-López, M. A., and F. J. López-Escudero. 2005. Resistencia y suseptibilidad a la verticilosis. In L. Rallo, et. al, eds., Variedades de olivo en España (Libro II: Variabilidad y selección). Madrid: Junta de Andalucía, MAPA y Ediciones Mundi-Prensa.

Civantos López-Villalta, M. 1999. Olive pest and disease management. Madrid: International Olive Oil Council.

Daane, K. M., R. E. Rice, F. G. Zalom, W. W. Barnett, and W. M. Johnson. 2005. Arthropod pests of olives. In G. S. Sibbett and L. Ferguson, eds., Olive production manual. 2nd ed. Oakland: University of California Agriculture and Natural Resources Publication 3353. 105–114.

Grafton-Cardwell, B., and K. Godfrey. 2005. Liquid-sugar ant bait stations are nearing registration for agricultura. UCCE Topics in Subtropics Newsletter 4(1): 2–3.

Krueger, W. H., M. N. Shroth, and B. L. Teviotdale. 1999. Improvements in the control of olive knot disease. Acta Horticulturae 474:467–571.

López-Escudero, F. J., C. del Rio, J. M. Caballero, and M. A. Blanco-López. 2004. Evaluation of olive cultivars for resistance to Verticillium dahliae. European Journal of Plant Pathology 110:79–85.

O'Malley, K., J. Bentivoglio, C. Beckingham, and D. Conlan. 2003. Organic olive management: A guide for Australian olive growers. Pendle Hill: New South Wales Agriculture and Australian Olive Association.

Peñalver, R., A. Garcia, J. Pérez-Panadés, C. Del Rio, J. M. Caballero, J. Pinochet, J. Piquer, E. A. Carbonell, and M. Milagros López. 2005. Resistencia y susceptibilidad a la tuberculosis variedades de olivo en españa. Madrid: Junta de Andalucia, M.A.P.A. y Ediciones Mundi-Prensa.

Rallo, L., D. Barranco, J. M. Caballero, C. Del Rio, A. Martin, J. Tous, and I. Trujillo. 2005. Variedades de olivo en españa. Madrid: Junta de Andalucia, M.A.P.A. y Ediciones Mundi-Prensa.

Sibbett, G. S. and L. Ferguson, eds. 2005. Olive production manual. 2nd ed. Oakland: University of California Agriculture and Natural Resources Publication 3353.

Sibbett, G. S., J. E. Dibble, and J. D. Babcock. 1976. Black scale now a major olive pest. California Agriculture 30(11): 12–13.

Teviotdale, B. L. 2005. Diseases of olive. In G. S. Sibbett and L. Ferguson, eds., Olive production manual. 2nd ed. Oakland: University of California Agriculture and Natural Resources Publication 3353. 119–122.

Teviotdale, B. L., and W. H. Krueger. 2004. Effects of timing of copper sprays, defoliation, rainfall and innoculum concentration on incidence of olive knot disease. Plant Disease 88:131–135.

Teviotdale, B. L., G. S. Sibbert, and D. H. Harper. 1989. Several copper fungicides control olive leaf spot. California Agriculture 43(5): 30–31.

Trapero, A., and M. A. Blanco. 1997. Enfermedades. In El Cultivo del olivo. Madrid: Junta De Andalucia Consejeria de Agricultura y Pesca, Ediciones Mundi-Prensa. 460–507.

Trapero, A., and L. M. López-Doncel. 2005. Resistencia y susceptibilidad al repilo en variedades de olivo en españa. Madrid: Junta de Andalucia, M.A.P.A. y Ediciones Mundi-Prensa.

Van Steenwyk, R. A., L. Ferguson, and F. G. Zalom. 2004. UC pest management guidelines: Olives. Oakland: University of California Agriculture and Natural Resources Publication 3452. University of California Integrated Pest Management Web site, http://www.ipm.ucdavis.edu/PMG/r583301311.html.

8

Organic Weed Management in Olive Orchards

W. THOMAS LANINI AND PAUL M. VOSSEN

INTRODUCTION

Controlling weeds in organic farming systems requires combining the use of many techniques and strategies to achieve economically acceptable weed control and yields. Weeds can always be pulled or cut out, but the question is simply how much time and money a grower can spend to reduce weed pressure. The more a grower is able to reduce weed pressure (seed and perennial propagules) the more economical it is to produce crops (table 8.1).

Research indicates that without some form of weed control, crop yields and plant vigor will be greatly reduced. In organic farming, weed control is only one goal of a weed management system. A good organic weed management plan should present a minimum erosion risk, provide a "platform" for the movement of farm equipment, not adversely impact pest management or soil fertility, and minimize weed competition for water and nutrients. This chapter is an overview of some organically acceptable weed control practices available for common weeds in olive orchards. (For more information on identifying and managing weeds,

see *Weeds of California and Other Western States*, DiTomaso and Healy 2007).

If you choose not to use synthetic and systemic pesticides, you should go the extra distance to try to keep the orchard as clean as possible. Techniques that reduce the contribution of seeds to the weed seed bank over time also reduce weed pressure and can contribute to reduced weeding costs. Ideally, no weed should be allowed to go to seed because buried seeds create weed problems for many years in the future. As an example, seed of common purslane (*Portulaca oleracea*) has been shown to remain viable for over 20 years in the soil, while black mustard (*Brassica nigra*) seed survives for over 40 years. The longevity of weed seed in combination with the large numbers of seed produced by individual plants (i.e., 100,000 per plant for large purslane or barnyardgrass [*Echinochloa crus-galli*] plants) can lead to long-term buildup of enormous seed banks in the soil.

Perennial weeds can be especially difficult to manage organically if they are allowed to become well established. Perennials are able to reproduce vegetatively as well as by seed in most cases. Perennial weeds commonly found in olive orchards include ber-

Table 8.1. Effects of various orchard floor management strategies on shoot length and trunk diameter

Treatment	Shoot length increase		Trunk diameter increase	
	in	cm	in	cm
wood chip mulch	6.0	15.3	2.1	5.3
weed fabric (black synthetic)	4.8	12.2	1.9	4.7
herbicide (bare ground)	4.4	11.1	1.6	4.3
cultivation (bare ground)	3.5	8.9	1.7	4.4
resident weeds, mowed	2.6	6.7	1.3	3.3

mudagrass, johnsongrass, field bindweed, and yellow nutsedge (see the sections at the end of this chapter). Establishing a policy of regular monitoring and control of weeds can be useful. Careful weed management during the season and during the off season can be helpful as well.

MULCHES

One control method is through the use of organic mulch. The mulch blocks light, preventing weed germination or growth. Many materials can be used as mulches including plastics or organic materials such as municipal yard waste, wood chips, straw, hay, sawdust, and newspaper (plate 8.1). Disposal of plastic mulches still remains a problem, as most plastic mulches are either removed and taken to a landfill or degrade and litter the area around the orchard with pieces of plastic.

To be effective, mulch must block all light to the weeds. Different mulch materials vary in the depth necessary to accomplish this. Organic mulches must be maintained in a layer 4 inches (10 cm) or more thick. Organic mulches break down with time, and the original thickness typically reduces by 60 percent after 1 year.

Cover crops are sometimes grown in olive orchards to compete with weeds for resources, reducing weed abundance or growth. (More information of the use of cover crops in orchards is available at http://www.sarep.ucdavis.edu/ccrop/index.htm; see also Ingels et al. 1998 for related information.) Cover crops can be grown in the middles, and in the spring, a "mow-and-throw" mower can be used to cut the cover crops and throw them as mulch into the tree rows (plate 8.2). This works well if the mulch layer is thick. Weeds that emerge through the mulch can be controlled using an organic contact herbicide or hand-weeding.

The additional benefits of mulches are significant. Mulch conserves moisture by reducing evaporation. Soil temperature is better maintained and organic material is added to the soil on breakdown. Weed germination is greatly impeded and growth diminished. Some grasses will survive the mulching but are shallow-rooted and can be easily pulled out. Partially rotted straw or hay that is not otherwise of use can be used as mulch, but it must come from fields that have not used pesticides or chemical fertilizers. Perennial weeds sprouting from established propagules can generally penetrate organic mulches. However, black plastic mulches can stop most herbaceous perennials, but nutsedge (*Cyperus* spp.) and blackberry (*Rubus*

spp.) can penetrate plastic mulches. Bermudagrass will often grow from the sides of plastic mulches.

ORGANICALLY ACCEPTABLE HERBICIDES

In recent years, several organic, contact-type herbicide products have appeared on the market. These include the clove oil products such as Matran EC (produced by EcoSmart) and acetic acid or citric acid products such as AllDown (produced by Summerset). These products damage any green vegetation contacted, including the leaves and young stems of olive trees, but they are safe if they are applied directly to woody stems and trunks. Because these herbicides kill only contacted tissue, good coverage is essential. Adding an organically acceptable surfactant is recommended. Because these materials lack residual activity, repeat applications will be needed to control new flushes of weeds.

Food-grade acetic acid (vinegar) is organically acceptable and controls small annual weeds when used as a soil supplement. The higher the concentration of acetic acid, the better it works, although food-grade acetic acid is typically 8 percent acetic acid or less (pickling acetic acid is closer to 15 percent). Repeat treatments are often necessary as there is no residual activity. Generally, vegetation is sprayed until wet, which may require high volumes if weed density is high.

Another organic herbicide that has appeared on the market in the last few years is corn gluten meal, which is sold under many trade names. It is expensive and has failed to provide even minimal weed control in the vast majority of California trials. Organic herbicides are expensive at this time and may not be cost-effective for commercial orchard production. Finally, approval by one's organic certifier should also be checked in advance, as use of these alternative herbicides is not cleared by all agencies. The efficacy of all these materials is much less than synthetic herbicides, and they do not control established perennial weeds.

CULTIVATION

Cultivation is the most widely used method of weed control in organic systems (plate 8.3). Mechanical cultivation uproots or buries weeds. Weed burial works best on small weeds, while larger weeds are better controlled by destroying the root-shoot connection or by slicing, cutting, or turning the soil to separate the root system from contact with the soil. Cultivation is effective for summer and winter annual weeds, but it is not as effective against summer perennial weeds like johnsongrass, nutsedge, bermudagrass, and field bindweed.

In most orchards, cultivation is limited to the orchard middles because the presence of permanent sprinklers or raised berms preclude cross-cultivation. Close or deep cultivation should be avoided to minimize the risk of injury to the olive root and crown, which can lead to crown gall disease. Shallow in-row cultivation also helps avoid bringing more weed seeds near the surface to germinate (plate 8.4).

Night tillage may help to reduce weed germination according to an Oregon study (Scopel et al. 1994). Many weeds require a flash of red light that is microseconds in duration in order to germinate. It is thought that weed seeds get this flash when suspended in soil during tillage. In the Oregon study, a 4- to 5-fold enhancement of weed germination can occur from exposure to light as in daylight tilling. After night tilling, only seeds left on the soil surface will germinate, which still can be quite a few. Because some seeds are always left on the soil surface, it may take several tillage passes to obtain much effect. Regardless of whether it works or not, at worst you just lose a little sleep. The Oregon study showed that most summer annual weeds like pigweed (*Amaranthus* spp.), lambsquarters (*Chenopodium album*), and barnyardgrass respond favorably to night tillage, as do many winter annual species.

WEEDER GEESE

Geese have been used for weed management in a large number of crops for many years (plate 8.5). All types of geese will graze weeds. There is considerable literature citing their use in strawberries and occasional mention of usage in orchards. Investigators at Michigan State University studied the impacts of populations of domestic geese and chickens in a nonchemical orchard system; geese were observed to feed heavily on weeds, especially grasses (Clark et al. 1995).

Geese prefer grass species and will eat other weeds and crops only after the grasses are gone and they become hungry. If confined, they will even dig up and eat rhizomes of johnsongrass and bermudagrass. They appear to have a particular preference for bermudagrass and johnsongrass, weeds that can be especially troublesome in orchards.

Care must be exercised when using geese to avoid placing them near any grass crops, such as corn, sorghum, small grains, and so on, as these species are their preferred food. Geese also require water for drinking, shade during hot weather, and protection from dogs and other predators. Portable fencing helps keep them in the area you want them to work and also keeps predators out. Young geese work best, as their major interests are eating and sleeping. Some people who have used weeder geese have complained of the excessive honking noise they can make.

Although geese are mentioned in this chapter, other animals such as sheep or goats can also be used. Sheep eat almost all weeds down to ground level, which reduces competition but does not eliminate it. Goats are browsers and must be carefully managed to avoid damage to trees.

FLAME WEEDING

Flamers can be used for weed control, with propane-fueled models being most common. Heat causes the cell sap of plants to expand, rupturing the cell walls; this process occurs in most plant tissues at about 130°F (54.5°C). Weeds must have fewer than two true leaves for greatest burning efficiency. Grasses are harder to kill by flaming because the growing point is below the ground. After flaming, weeds that have been killed change from a glossy to a matte finish. This occurs very rapidly in most cases. Foliage that retains a thumbprint when pressure is applied between your thumb and finger has been adequately flamed. Typically, flaming can be done at 3 to 5 miles per hour (5 to 8 km/hr) through orchards, although this depends on the heat output of the unit being used. Repeated flaming can likewise be used to suppress perennial weeds such as field bindweed. Care must be taken to avoid igniting dry vegetation, which could injure the trees or start a wildfire.

The specific flaming angle, flaming pattern, and flame length vary with the manufacturer's recommendations. They range from 30° to 40° at 8 to 12 inches (21 to 31 cm) above the base of the plants, with flame lengths of approximately 12 to 15 inches (31 to 38 cm) (plate 8.6).

Best results are obtained under windless conditions, as winds can prevent the heat from reaching the target. Early morning or evening is the best time to observe the flame for adjustment. Flame Engineering, Inc., and Thermal Weed Control Systems, Inc., manufacture both hand- and tractor-mounted flame-weeding equipment.

In a study comparing control of weeds by flaming, species and growth stage were the most important variables (Ascard 1995). One weed which was resistant to flaming was cheeseweed (*Malva neglecta*), with little or no control. To control annual weeds at later developmental stages (more than six true leaves), a single-pass flame treatment was not sufficient. For lambsquarters, three subsequent treatments were necessary for 95 percent control. For the flame control of dandelion (*Taraxacum officinalis*), the developmental stage is also crucial. Small plants were killed by one flaming, while bigger plants often survived four flamings (69% control). For flame-tolerant or perennial weeds, only 76 percent weed reduction was achieved after four treatments. In an orchard with mainly annual weeds, three treatments controlled 95 percent of weeds. Flame weeding is often associated with problems such as high energy consumption, low driving speed, and irregular weed control.

Another alternative for nonchemical weed control is based on hot steam. High-temperature water provides a form of thermal weed control, yet eliminates the danger of flame application in arid regions where open fires are a hazard. Two companies, Waipuna Systems, Ltd., from New Zealand, and Aqua Heat, from Minneapolis (which may no longer be in business), have developed equipment that delivers superheated water from a boom or spray nozzle attached to a diesel-fired boiler. The high pressure and hot water damages the cellular structure and kills weeds within several hours or a few days. The first signs of the effectiveness are change of leaf color and plant withering. In general, steam has been shown to be less effective than flaming. Even with a temperature of 450°C (842°F) the steam was not able to control all weeds. Factors affecting the use of steam were age of weeds, slow application speed, amount of steam applied, and cost of fuel.

WEED MAPPING

Weed distribution is not uniform; patches of weeds, particularly perennials, should be managed individually. A global positioning system (GPS) unit can be used to map the population and treatment can be made to that area at a lower cost than treating the whole orchard. By mapping the weed patches, follow-up evaluations can be made and further treatments applied as needed.

SPECIAL WEED PROBLEMS

Bermudagrass (*Cynodon dactylon*) is a vigorous, warm-season perennial. It expands rapidly with an extensive system of rhizomes and stolons, which can form new plants after being cut by cultivation. Seed also help bermudagrass expand to new locations. Bermudagrass competes in olive orchards for moisture and nutrients.

Johnsongrass (*Sorghum halapense*) is also a warm-season perennial grass that spreads from seed or from an extensive rhizome system. It can overtop small trees and is highly competitive for light, moisture, and nutrients. Repeated cultivations can suppress the growth of either johnsongrass or bermudagrass but may also spread these weeds. Geese will eat these grass species and if left to forage in an infested area will dig out most of the stolons and rhizomes.

Yellow nutsedge (*Cyperus esculentus*) is a perennial weed that reproduces from underground tubers. Viable seed are rarely produced. A single plant can produce hundreds of new tubers in a single year, with tubers able to survive for 2 to 5 years in the soil. Each tuber contains several buds, and each bud is capable of producing a plant. Generally, only a single bud grows from a tuber, but if the tuber is destroyed by cultivation, a new bud is activated. Repeated cultivation at 3-week intervals destroys successive flushes of nutsedge and eventually kills the tuber. Geese do not eat nutsedge.

Field bindweed (*Convolvulus arvensis*) is a vigorous perennial weed. It grows from seed and also from rhizomes and extensive, deep roots. Field bindweed seed has been known to survive for over 30 years. Because of the longevity of the seed in the soil, it is critical to destroy plants before they can produce seed. The plants may spread from stem or root sections that are cut during cultivations, but cultivation controls seedlings. As with nutsedge, repeated cultivations at 2- to 3-week intervals depletes the carbohydrates in the root system and eventually kills these weeds. Longer periods between cultivations can allow the energy reserves in the roots to recover.

REFERENCES

Ascard, J. 1995. Effects of flame weeding on weed species at different developmental stages. Weed Research 35(5): 397–411.

Clark, M. S., S. H. Gage, L. B. DeLind, and M. Lennington. 1995. The compatibility of domestic birds with a nonchemical agroecosystem. American Journal of Alternative Agriculture 10(3): 114–120.

DiTomaso, J. M., and E. A. Healy. 2007. Weeds of California and other western states. 2 vols. Oakland: University of California Agriculture and Natural Resources Publication 3488.

Ingels, C. A., R. L. Bugg, G. T. McGourty, and L. P. Christensen, eds. 1998. Cover cropping in vineyards: A grower's handbook. Oakland: University of California Agriculture and Natural Resources Publication 3338.

Johnson, C. 1960. Management of weeder geese in commercial fields. California Agriculture (Aug.): 5.

Kolberg, R. L., and L. J. Wiles. 2002. Effect of steam application on cropland weeds. Weed Technology 16(1): 43–49.

Scopel, A. L., C. L. Ballare, and S. R. Radosevich. 1994. Photostimulation of seed germination during soil tillage. New Phytologist 126(1): 145–152.

Tworkoski, T. 2002. Herbicide effects of essential oils. Weed Science 50(4): 425–431.

EQUIPMENT SUPPLIERS AND SOURCES OF INFORMATION

Propane Flamers

Red Dragon Products and Services, http://www.flameengineering.com./GP_Flamers.html

Thermoweed (United Kingdom), http://www.thermoweed.com/orchards.htm

Weed Control B.V. (Netherlands), http://www.ecoflame.nl/Ecoflame/mb_onkruid_en.htm

Steam Weeders

Waipuna (New Zealand), http://www.waipuna.co.nz/

In-row Cultivators and Other Weed Controls

Clemens Maschinefabrik (Germany), http://www.clemens-online.com/index.EN.php?cnt=p4000&nav=m203

Gearmore Inc., http://www.gearmore.com/

Green Hoe Co., Inc., http://www.greenhoecompany.com/

KIMCO Manufacturing, http://www.kimcomfg.com/9300.html

McConkey, http://www.mcconkeyco.com/pdf/WovenShade.pdf

Weed Badger, http://www.weedbadger.com/

Weed Seeker, http://www.ntechindustries.com/

Middles Tillage

T. G. Schemiser Co., Inc., http://www.tgschmeiser.com/ptm.html

Organic Herbicides

Iowa State University Extension Corn Gluten Meal Research Site, http://www.gluten.iastate.edu/

Scentoils, http://scentoils.com/

Summerset Products, http://www.sumrset.com/spec_sheet.htm

USDA Agricultural Research Service Sustainable Agriculture Systems Laboratory Web site, http://www.ars.usda.gov/main/site_main.htm?modecode=12-65-04-00

Geese

Metzer Farms, http://www.metzerfarms.com/

Part 4
Composting and
Olive Waste Management

9

Agricultural Use of Olive Oil Mill Wastes

JEFFREY A. CREQUE

INTRODUCTION

Less than one tenth of one percent of the world's olive oil is produced in the United States, and almost all of that is produced in California. Recent growth in domestic demand for premium olive oil suggests that the acreage of olives for oil production in California will inevitably expand. It is essential for the success of this emerging agricultural industry and for the ecological integrity of California's agricultural landscapes that environmentally appropriate methods of on-farm use of olive oil processing wastes be identified and adopted. To succeed, these methods must maximize the agroecological benefits of on-farm recycling of this nutrient- and carbon-rich material while avoiding the serious environmental problems historically associated with olive oil production in Europe and the Middle East.

Characteristics of olive oil mill waste (OMW) vary with the type of extraction system used. Three-phase centrifugal extractors produce fruitwater, a somewhat dry paste and oil. Two-phase centrifugal extractors produce a wet paste and oil. Presses are three-phase systems, and produce fruitwater, a very dry press cake, and oil. Finally, wash waters from mill cleaning operations are also a component of the OMW stream. Throughout this chapter, the paste fraction of the waste stream is referred to as solid OMW (SOMW), while fruitwater and wash waters, typically combined for disposal, are here referred to together as liquid OMW (LOMW).

Disposal of both liquid and solid OMW remains one of the most serious environmental problems in the Mediterranean region. Direct soil application has been considered an inexpensive means of disposing of OMW and recovering its agronomically beneficial mineral and organic components. However, the high organic acid and phenol contents of this material, with their high oxygen (O_2) and nitrogen (N) demands and

significant water pollution potential, can render direct soil application particularly problematic. This is especially true where available land area is small relative to waste volume and where slopes or soils are unsuitable. The need to store large volumes of liquid wastes through the rainy season, when most of it is produced and during which time handling and land application is most difficult, further complicates OMW disposal.

Traditionally, the small size and wide distribution of Mediterranean olive mills led to OMW being spread in relatively low volumes over large areas of land. Beginning in the 1950s, the centralization of olive oil production in large, industrialized facilities and the widespread adoption of continuous centrifugation extraction systems employing large volumes of process water led to huge quantities of olive waste being discharged directly to waterways and the sea. Because of severe negative impacts on aquatic ecosystems, this practice is now illegal in the European Union (EU) and has been replaced primarily by the use of evaporation ponds and subsequent land disposal of the residual sludge.

Excessive use of OMW sludge from evaporation ponds, however, immobilizes soil N, inhibits crop growth, and reduces soil biological activity. Consequently, use of untreated OMW sludge as an agricultural soil amendment is strictly limited under European Economic Community (EEC) directives. Despite this increase in regulation, environmental problems associated with OMW disposal in the Mediterranean region continue because of the concentration of large volumes of this material on relatively small land areas and the indirect discharge of waste into waterways as a result of overloading of soils and subsequent wet-season runoff.

Despite the serious environmental problems associated with inappropriate OMW disposal methods, it is important to recognize that OMW is both biodegradable and of significant potential value to the agroecosystems from which it is derived. After all,

OMW consists of crushed olives and water, with one of the more biochemically problematic elements—the oil itself—removed. Appropriately, therefore, much recent research has focused on strategies for beneficial agricultural use and recycling of OMW. In recent years, successful strategies have included carefully controlled direct land application of OMW as well as composting of OMW followed by agricultural and horticultural use of the finished product.

．．
DIRECT LAND APPLICATION

Olive oil is composed of carbon, hydrogen, and oxygen derived from atmospheric carbon dioxide (CO_2) and water (H_2O). As such, the export of olive oil from the agricultural ecosystem does not in and of itself deplete soil nutrient reserves. This suggests the potential for olive oil production systems to be ecologically sustainable indefinitely. Removal of olive oil production wastes from the farm, however, not only results in the potential for environmental pollution, but also means the loss of nutrients necessary for the continued productivity of olive orchard soils. Ideally, from the perspective of environmental quality and agricultural sustainability, olive oil production wastes should be returned to the soils from which they originate.

Direct land application of waste materials is suitable under the following conditions (Fuller and Warrick 1985):

- The wastes are biodegradable.

- Indigenous soil microbiota will survive and continue to function at practical waste application rates.

- Long-term toxic effects do not occur or can be readily mitigated.

- Practical application rates will not pollute groundwater or surface water, or allow toxic substances to enter the food chain.

- Land disposal is cost effective.

- Soil productivity will be unchanged or improved.

- Site soil, climatic, topographical, and hydrogeological characteristics are compatible with the nature, rate, and schedule of waste application.

Direct soil application of both solid and liquid OMW has been the most common and inexpensive method to dispose of these materials and recover their beneficial mineral and organic components. Because of the high content of phenols and polyphenols—long-chain carbon molecules that tend to decompose very slowly in the soil environment—direct land application can result in the immobilization of soil nitrogen and oxygen by soil microbes. This has negative impacts on plant growth in the receiving soils, commonly referred to as phytotoxic effects.

Nevertheless, direct application of LOMW to land at rates of less than 3 inches per acre (<762 m³/ha) has long been practiced with beneficial effects on soil fertility, soil microbial populations, nitrogen fixation, soil stability, and crop yields. Even at seven to eight times this rate, soil nitrogen has been found to increase above levels that could be explained by OMW additions alone (Cabrera et al. 1996). This suggests that OMW is capable of stimulating nitrogen fixation by soil bacteria, despite the well-documented bactericidal characteristics of this material. Even at such high application rates, nitrate-nitrogen was found to increase to levels common in agricultural soils, and no nitrate was observed to leach from the upper soil profile.

LOMW applied to the soils of young olive groves at the very modest rates of 0.09 to 0.7 inches per acre (23 to 178 m³/ha) had no negative effect on tree growth or soil chemistry or biology, but did increase olive tree shoot growth relative to that on untreated soils (Marsilio et al. 1990). A number of researchers have reported a significant increase in free-living N-fixing microflora in OMW-treated soils, as well as an increase in soil nitrogen (Balis et al. 1996; Cabrera et al. 1996; Chatjipavlidis et al. 1996; Fiorelli et al. 1996). Increases in aerobic cellulose-decomposing bacteria have also been observed. Direct application of LOMW at the rate of 1, 2 and 3 inches per acre (254, 508 and 762 m³/ha) had no lasting effect on total seasonal biomass production of resident vegetation on a Yorkville clay loam in Marin County, California (Creque 1998). Despite obvious differences in plant growth among treatments during early phases of the experiment, no significant differences in biomass production were found among treatments. Practical considerations arising from the difficulty of applying larger amounts of liquid waste to these soils after the onset of fall rains (typical of the olive oil milling season in California) led to the selection of 1 inch (25 mm) as the recommended LOMW application rate on this site. LOMW can be contained in tanks, ponds, or mixed with dry bulking agents to prevent movement away from the site (plate 9.1).

Despite potential problems of phytotoxicity, nitrogen immobilization, nutrient leaching, and inhibition of soil microflora commonly associated with direct application of large volumes of both liquid and solid

OMW to agricultural soils, direct land application of OMW is technically and economically feasible. With proper attention to volume and rates of application, weather, soil, slope and cover crop conditions, and allowance for appropriate buffers around sensitive areas such as streams and ponds, direct land application is a viable means of OMW utilization. In California, these applications are regulated by the regional water quality control boards (RWQCB) under a discharge permit or waiver (for more information on the RWQCBs, see http://www.waterboards.ca.gov/regions.html).

···

OLIVE OIL MILL WASTE COMPOSTING

Composting is receiving increasing attention throughout the international olive oil industry as an agroecologically appropriate method of both solid and liquid OMW recycling and is now considered the most suitable strategy for recycling OMW nutrients to croplands. Composting addresses the problems of phytotoxicity, nutrient leaching, and inhibition of microflora commonly associated with direct application of large volumes of OMW to agricultural soils. Currently, on-farm composting in California is regulated by local enforcement agencies (often by county health departments), under California Integrated Waste Management Board (CIWMB) guidelines, and on certified organic farms by National Organic Program (NOP) standards (see NOP 2001).

Composting is a biological process that results in the transformation of organic materials to compost, a relatively biochemically stable material of widely recognized agronomic value. Because of its biochemical stability, mature OMW compost is not phytotoxic. Compost maturity refers to the degree of completion of the composting process. Compost at intermediate stages of decomposition may contain phytotoxic compounds, including organic acids and polyphenols. Additionally, high rates of microbial activity in immature compost require large amounts of both oxygen and nitrogen. As with uncomposted OMW, therefore, immature composts applied to soils tend to cause soil biota to draw both oxygen and nitrogen from the surrounding soil in order to biodegrade this material. Because soil biota are much more effective at oxygen and nitrogen utilization than is the growing crop, the crop is typically left starved of both.

Under properly controlled composting conditions, pathogens are destroyed by both heat and biophagy (consumption by other compost microbes), and phytotoxic organic materials are transformed to benign forms. Controlled composting enables correction of imbalances in the raw materials, or feedstock, and manipulation of the aerobic decomposition process to achieve specific effects. For example, mixing OMW low in available nitrogen with high-nitrogen materials (such as livestock manures) permits adjustment of the feedstock carbon to nitrogen (C:N) ratio to that needed for thermophilic (high-temperature) aerobic composting to occur. Once the properly managed composting process is complete, mature OMW compost can be safely and beneficially applied to soils in quantities well above those appropriate for unprocessed OMW.

The past two decades have seen considerable investigation into the potential for composting to address the growing need for biodegradation and agronomic utilization of OMW, and recent trends suggest composting is becoming an increasingly accepted method of handling both solid and liquid OMW. Biochemical transformation of OMW through composting has been shown to result in a desirable increase in pH, a rise in nitrogen concentration, a decline in the C:N ratio, and a decline in electrical conductivity (EC). While OMW contains a wide range of phytotoxic compounds, with additional phytotoxic factors often formed during the composting process itself, these are effectively absent in mature compost.

Because of the high content of polyphenols and low levels of available nitrogen in OMW, direct land application can result in virtually complete immobilization of soil nitrogen reserves. This in turn has negative implications for plant growth in the receiving soils and accounts for much of the reported phytotoxic effects of OMW. While reported C:N ratios of OMW vary from very high (100:1) to levels ideal for composting (25:1), the lignaceous (woodlike) character of OMW polyphenols and the resulting low availability of nitrogen in these wastes render additional nitrogen essential for successful composting of OMW.

While the water content of OMW varies with processing methods, the waste stream typically consists of both a liquid and a paste with a moisture content of 50 to 70 percent or more. As a result, an absorbent bulking material, such as straw, wood shavings, shredded paper, etc., must be added to achieve adequate aeration and obtain the ideal compost moisture level of 50 to 60 percent. OMW has been co-composted with vine prunings, olive branches, olive husks, and maize stover. While some of these materials may effectively absorb OMW moisture, they are themselves high-carbon materials, increasing the need for additional high-nitrogen compost additives, such as cotton mill wastes, sewage sludge, or poultry manures. Other bulking agents and additives employed in OMW composting have included urban green waste, wood chips, wood shaving–based stable manures, and dairy manure, as well as olive leaves, urea, grape pomace, and goat manure.

Active composting generates heat and releases water vapor that can eventually dry the material, limiting further biological activity (plate 9.2). If this occurs, LOMW can be added directly to the compost pile to maintain moisture needed for biological activity. Certified organic farms must be careful to select additives in accordance with NOP regulations. Care should also be taken to select materials that will prevent high salt loads (high EC) in the finished compost.

In summary, desirable characteristics of materials for co-composting with OMW include high-cellulose, low-lignin bulking agents; low-salinity (low-EC), high-nitrogen additives as needed to achieve optimal C:N (Rynk 1992); and acid to neutral pH conditions to minimize nitrogen losses via volatilization during composting. Livestock bedding materials, including manure, shavings, and straw, can often be obtained cheaply or free of charge in agricultural regions; they provide a good mix of bulking agent and nitrogen, while manures or green wastes can provide additional nitrogen. While SOMW typically ranges between 25 to 50 percent of the initial OMW compost feedstock, experimentation using readily available free or low-cost materials is recommended to determine optimal ratios for co-composting on a case-by-case basis. Finally, high-nitrogen feedstocks and additives, such as manures and cotton wastes, are usually preferable to lower-nitrogen materials, such as wood chips or bedding manures, to facilitate complete biodegradation of OMW in the compost environment.

Evaluation of Compost Maturity

The importance of compost maturity depends on its use. Compost for nursery applications, such as potting soils or similar planting media, must be sufficiently biochemically stable to support germination and growth of seeds and seedlings. In contrast, compost applied as a light surface dressing, for example, into an orchard cover crop, can usually complete the maturation process in situ without negative impact on plant growth. Certified organic producers must comply with NOP standards pertaining to manure-based composts. However, these standards are designed to ensure that compost made with livestock manures is pathogen-free at the time of crop harvest and do not ensure compost maturity.

A variety of criteria have been employed to determine completion of the OMW composting process and suitability of OMW compost for use. These include bioassay, germination index, and other chemical and biological indices, such as C:N ratios, cation exchange capacity (CEC), humus content and quality, and respiration. The U.S. Composting Council has developed widely adopted industry standards for compost maturity, depending on purpose of use.

Bioassays offer a simple on-farm means of evaluating compost maturity. However, seed germination indices and early growth of seedlings may not be adequate indicators of compost maturity, despite their widespread use in this capacity. Lack of nitrogen availability may not be immediately apparent in early-stage bioassays, and monitoring plant growth for a period of at least 4 to 6 weeks following germination is recommended. Compost-soil-plant nitrogen dynamics may be a more important limiting factor in the use of OMW compost than the level of phytotoxic compounds. A prolonged maturation or curing phase beyond temperature stabilization may be needed before OMW compost is safe for use at sensitive stages of plant growth or where the compost is incorporated into the soil rather than applied as a surface dressing or mulch.

SUMMARY AND CONCLUSIONS

Disposal of olive mill solid and liquid wastes has become environmentally problematic due to the nature of the material and the large volumes produced under centralized processing scenarios in the Mediterranean region. However, where volumes are small relative to available land area and site conditions allow, on-farm disposal of OMW is agroecologically appropriate (plate 9.3).

The solid fraction of the olive oil extraction waste stream, consisting of olive pomace and leaves, constitutes 30 to 60 percent of the total OMW, depending on moisture content. This is readily processed on-farm, using standard aerobic windrow composting methods. OMW composting results in biochemical transformation of phytotoxic elements in the waste to benign compounds, while requiring low-density bulking agents, high-nitrogen additives, and a sufficient maturation period, depending on the horticultural or agricultural end use of the compost. Evaporative losses of water are accelerated as a result of the high temperatures associated with aerobic composting, further assisting with waste volume reduction.

The liquid fraction of OMW, consisting of both fruitwater and wash water, can be used to maintain desired moisture levels during composting or applied directly to agricultural soils under carefully controlled conditions. Provision of a vegetated buffer around ponds and stream channels is essential, and under no circumstances should liquid wastes be applied to saturated soils or during rainfall. Direct solid or liquid OMW contact with the foliage and bark of young olive trees should be avoided. Application rates must be evaluated on a site-specific basis and vary with slope, soil, vegetation cover, and climatic conditions. Rates of from 0.5 to 3 inches (12.5 to 75 mm) or approximately 13,500 to 81,000 gallons per acre (126 to 758 m³/ha) have been found to be both practical to apply and to have no long-term negative effect on olive tree or cover crop growth, while promoting beneficial changes in numerous soil quality indicators. Liquid OMW is not suitable for application through drip irrigation systems due to the relatively high oil and solid content, both of which will quickly clog emitters.

A growing body of literature and on-farm experience strongly support the conclusion that, where sufficient land area is available, on-farm use of OMW is agroecologically beneficial and environmentally preferable to off-site disposal. A combination of direct soil application and composting of liquid wastes, along with composting of solid wastes, offers a flexible, economical, and agroecologically appropriate approach to using these problematic, yet agronomically valuable, materials.

· ·

ACKNOWLEDGMENTS

The author gratefully acknowledges the generous support of Mrs. Nan Tucker McEvoy, McEvoy Ranch and McEvoy of Marin, LLC., in making this chapter possible.

· ·

REFERENCES

Abu-Zreig, M., and M. Al-Widyan. 2002. Influence of olive mills solid waste on soil hydraulic properties. Communications in Soil Science and Plant Analysis 33(3–4): 505–517.

Amirante, P., and A. Montervino. 1996. Treatment of olive oil mill waste by thermal reduction and composting of the concentrate: Working experience in Apulia. Olivae 63:64–69.

Angelidaki, I., and B. K. Ahring. 1997. Codigestion of olive oil mill wastewaters with manure, household waste or sewage sludge. Biodegradation 8:221–226.

Arredondo-Moreno, T., and D. Johnson. 1998. Clipping effects on root architecture and morphology of 3 range grasses. Journal of Range Management 51(2): 207–213.

Balis, C., J. Chatjipavlidis, and F. Flouri. 1996. Olive mill waste as a substrate for nitrogen fixation. International Biodeterioration and Biodegradation 38(3–4): 169–178.

Benitez, E., R. Melgar, and R. Nogales. 2004. Estimating soil resilience to a toxic organic waste by measuring enzyme activities. Soil Biology and Biochemistry 36:1615–1623.

Cabrera, F., R. Lopez, A. Martinez-Bordiu, E. Dupuy de Lome, and J. M. Murillo. 1996. Land treatment of olive oil mill wastewater. International Biodeterioration and Biodegradation 38(3–4): 215–225.

Capasso, R. et al. 1995. Antibacterial polyphenols from olive oil mill waste waters. Journal of Applied Bacteriology 79:393–398.

Cayuela, M. L., M. A. Sanchez-Monedero, J. Molina, and A. Roig. 2005. Compost production from olive oil processing. Biocycle 46(2): 64–65.

Cegarra, J., C. Paredes, A. Roig, M. P. Bernal, and D. Garcia. 1996. Use of olive mill wastewater compost for crop production. International Biodeterioration and Biodegradation 38(3–4): 193–203.

Cegarra, J., J. A. Alburquerque, J. Gonzalvez, and D. Garcia. 2004. Composting of two-phase olive pomace. Olivae 101:12–15.

Chatjipavlidis, I., M. Antonakou, D. Demou, F. Flouri, and C. Balis. 1996. Bio-fertilization of olive oil mills liquid wastes: The pilot plant in Messinia, Greece. International Biodeterioration and Biodegradation 38(3–4): 183–187.

CIWMB (California Integrated Waste Management Board). 2004a. CIWMB regulations, Title 14. CIWMB Web site, http://www.ciwmb.ca.gov/Regulations/Title14/default .htm#chapter3.

———. 2004b. Compost quality: Performance requirements. CIWMB Web site, http://www.ciwmb.ca.gov/Organics/ products/quality/needs.htm.

Creque, J. A. 1998. On-farm utilization of olive mill wastes. Unpublished report for McEvoy Ranch, Petaluma, CA.

Epstein, E. 1997. The science of composting. Lancaster, PA: Technomic Publishing.

Estaun, V., C. Calvet, J. M. Grases, and M. V. Pages. 1985. Chemical determination of fatty acids, organic acids and phenols during olive marc composting process. Acta Horticulturae 172:263–270.

Fiorelli, F., L. Pasetti and E. Galli. 1996. Fertility-promoting metabolites produced by *Azotobacter vinelandii* grown on olive-mill wastewaters. International Biodeterioration and Biodegradation 38(3–4): 165–168.

Fuller, W. H., and A. W. Warrick. 1985. Soils in waste treatment and utilization. Boca Raton, FL: CRC Press.

Garcia-Gomez, A., A. Roig, and M. P. Bernal. 2003. Composting of the solid fraction of olive mill wastewater with olive leaves: Organic matter degradation and biological activity. Bioresource Technology 86:59–64.

Gonzalez, L., E. Bellido, and C. Benitez. 1994. Reduction of total polyphenols in olive mill wastewater by physicochemical purification. Journal of Environmental Science and Health A29(5): 851–865.

Loser, C., H. Ulbricht, and H. Seidel. 2004. Degradation of polycyclic aromatic hydrocarbons in waste wood. Compost Science and Utilization 12(4): 335–341.

Manios, V. I., P. E. Tsikalas, and H. I. Siminis. 1989. Phytotoxicity of olive tree leaf compost in relation to the organic acid concentration. Biological Wastes 27:307–317.

Mari, I., C. Ehaliotis, M. Kotsou, C. Balis, and D. Georgakakis. 2003. Respiration profiles in monitoring the composting of by-products from the olive oil agro-industry. Bioresource Technology 87:331–336.

Marsilio, V., L. Di Giovacchino, M. Solinas, N. Lombardo, and C. Briccoli-Bati. 1990. First observations on the disposal effects of olive oil mills vegetation waters on cultivated soil. Acta Horticulturae 286:493–496.

Monteoliva-Sanchez, M., C. Incerti, A. Ramos-Cormenzana, C. Paredes, A. Roig, and J. Cegarra. 1996. Study of the aerobic bacterial microbiota and the biotoxicity in various samples of olive mill wastewaters (alpechin) during their composting process. International Biodeterioration and Biodegradation 38(3–4): 211–214.

Mouncif, M., M. Faid, A. Achkari-Begdouri, and R. Lhadi. 1995. A biotechnological valorization and treatment of olive mill waste waters by selected yeast strains. Grasas y Aceites 46(6): 344–348.

Negro, M. J., and M. L. Solano. 1996. Laboratory composting assays of the solid residue resulting from the flocculation of oil mill wastewater with different lignocellulosic residues. Compost Science and Utilization 4(4): 62–71.

NOP (USDA National Organic Program). 2001. National Organic Program Product Handling Regulations Web site, http://www.ams.usda.gov/nop/NOP/standards/ProdHandReg.html.

Pages, M., V. Estaun, and C. Calvet. 1985. Physical and chemical properties of olive marc compost. Acta Horticulturae 172:271–276.

Papadimitriou, E. K., I. Chatjipavlidis, and C. Balis. 1997. Application of composting to olive mill wastewater treatment. Environmental Technology 18:101–107.

Papafotiou, M., M. Phsyhalou, G. Kargas, I. Chatzipavlidis, and J. Chronopoulos. 2004. Olive-mill wastes compost as growing medium component for the production of poinsettia. Scientia Horticulturae 102:167–175.

Paredes, C., M. P. Bernal, A. Roig, J. Cegarra, and M. A. Sanchez-Monedero. 1996. Influence of the bulking agent on the degradation of olive mill wastewater sludge during composting. International Biodeterioration and Biodegradation 38(3–4): 205–210.

Paredes, C., M. P. Bernal, J. Cegarra, and A. Roig. 2002. Bio-degradation of olive mill wastewater sludge by its co-composting with agricultural wastes. Bioresource Technology 85:1–8.

Perez, J. D., E. Esteban, and M. Gomez. 1986. Effects of wastewater from olive processing on seed germination and early plant growth of different vegetable species. Journal of Environmental Science and Health B21(4): 349–357.

Piperidou, C. I., C. I. Chaidou, C. D. Stalikas, K. Soulti, G. A. Pilidis, and C. Balis. 2000. Bioremediation of olive oil mill wastewater: Chemical alterations induced by Azotobacter vinelandii. Journal of Agricultural Food Chemistry 48(5): 1941–1948.

Pompei, R., M. G. Demontis, E. Sanjust, A. Rinaldi, and M. Ballero. 1994. Use of olive milling waste-water for the culture of mushrooms on perlite. Acta Horticulturae 361:179–185.

Ramos-Cormenzana, A., B. Juarez-Jimenez, and M. P. Garcia-Pareja. 1996. Antimicrobial activity of olive mill wastewaters (alpechin) and bio-transformed olive oil mill wastewater. International Biodeterioration and Biodegradation 38(3–4): 283–290.

Riffaldi, R., R. Levi-Minzi, A. Saviozzi, and G. Viti. 1997. Carbon mineralization potential of soils amended with sludge from olive processing. Bulletin of Environmental Contamination Toxicology 58:30–37.

Rozzi, A., and F. Malpei. 1996 Treatment and disposal of olive mill effluents. International Biodeterioration and Biodegradation 38(3–4): 135–144.

Rynk, R., ed. 1992. On-farm composting handbook. NRAES-54. Ithaca, NY: Natural Resource, Agriculture, and Engineering Service.

Sanchez-Monedero, M. A., J. Cegarra, D. Garcia, and A. Roig. 2002. Chemical and structural evolution of humic acids during organic waste composting. Biodegradation 13:361–371.

SCS (USDA Soil Conservation Service). 1985. Soil survey of Marin County. 1985-O-418–766. Washington, DC: Government Printing Office.

Sibbett, G. S., J. H. Connell, B. S. Luh, and L. Ferguson. 1994. Producing olive oil. In L. Ferguson, G. S. Sibbett, and G. C. Martin, eds., Olive production manual. Oakland: University of California Division of Natural Resources Publication 3353. 143–148.

Tomati, U., E. Galli, F. Fiorelli, and L. Pasetti. 1996. Fertilizers from composting of olive-mill wastewaters. International Biodeterioration and Biodegradation 38(3–4): 155–162.

Tomati, U., E. Madejon, and E. Galli, 2000. Evolution of humic acid molecular weight as an index of compost stability. Compost Science and Utilization 8(2): 108–115.

Tsioulpas, A. D., D. Dimou, D. Iconomou, and G. Aggelis. 2002. Phenolic removal in olive oil mill wastewater by strains of *Pleurotus* spp. in respect to their phenol oxidase (laccase) activity. Bioresource Technology 84:251–257.

USCC (United States Composting Council). 2002. Evaluating compost quality. USCC Web site, http://compostingcouncil.org/section.cfm?id=39.

———. 2005. Landscape architecture/design specifications for compost use. USCC Web site, http://compostingcouncil.org/pdf/LA_Specs_Program.pdf.

Van Herk, F. H., T. A. McAllister, C. L. Cockwill, N. Guselle, F. J. Larney, J. J. Miller, and M. E. Olson. 2004. Inactivation of *Giardia* cysts and *Cryptosporidium* oocysts in beef feedlot manure by thermophilic windrow composting. Compost Science and Utilization 12(3): 235–241.

Walker, D. J., and M. P. Bernal. 2004. Plant mineral nutrition and growth in a saline Mediterranean soil amended with organic wastes. Communications in Soil Science and Plant Analysis 35(17–18): 2495–2514.

Zucconi, F., A. Pera, M. Forte, and M. de Bertoldi. 1981. Evaluating toxicity of immature compost. Biocycle 22:54–57.

Part 5
Organic Certification

10

Agroecological Principles for Making the Conversion to Organic Olive Agroecosystems

STEPHEN R. GLIESSMAN

INTRODUCTION

Farmers have always had a reputation for being innovators and experimenters, willingly adopting new practices when they perceive that some benefit will be gained. This has been especially true in organic agriculture, where over the past 20 years creative farmers have made significant changes in farming that often challenged conventional wisdom on production practices, as well as the identity of agricultural products consumers are willing to buy. Remarkable increases in the area devoted to organic agriculture have been observed during the past decade (ERS 2005). In California alone, growth in annual organic sales and acres in production has averaged about 30 percent per year between 1992 and 2003 (Klonsky and Richter 2005). These growth trends support those that were predicted earlier (Swezey and Broome 2000).

While this transition occurs, we are constantly faced with the question of how sustainable these new agricultural systems really are. Sustainability in the broadest sense can be defined as farming systems that are ecologically sound, economically viable, and socially equitable and appropriate for all members of the food system, from growers to consumers (Gliessman 1998). But when we examine farming systems as ecological systems (more broadly known as agroecosystems) and use the science of agroecology for their design and management, we begin to realize that farmers and researchers must work together very closely to ensure that these new agroecosystems are not just trading one set of problems for others. Defined as the application of ecological concepts and principles to the design and management of sustainable agroecosystems (Gliessman 1998), agroecology offers a set of guiding principles for making sure that sustainability

is part of our framework while we make the conversion to organic production. Agroecologists are not satisfied with an approach that merely substitutes conventional inputs and practices with organically acceptable alternatives. They are not satisfied with an approach that is determined primarily by market demands and does not include the economic and social health of the agricultural communities in which food is produced—the economic well-being of farmers in particular is critical. And agroecologists are not satisfied with an approach that does not ensure food security for all consumers in all parts of the world. A much broader set of tools must be developed to evaluate the conversion process. Agroecology provides the ecological foundations for such an evaluation. We can apply these foundations as we develop organic olive systems.

PRINCIPLES GUIDING THE CONVERSION PROCESS

The process of conversion to organic production can be complex, requiring changes in field practices, new skill sets of farmers, day-to-day management of the farming operation, and changes in planning, marketing, and even philosophy (plate 10.1). The following ecological principles can serve as general guidelines for navigating the overall transformation (Gliessman 1998).

- Shift from throughflow nutrient management, where harvested nutrients are constantly brought in from outside sources, to recycling of nutrients, with increased dependence on natural processes such as biological nitrogen fixation and mycorrhizal relationships.

- Use renewable sources of energy, such as biodiesel, instead of nonrenewable sources.

- Eliminate the use of nonrenewable off-farm human inputs that have the potential to harm the environment or the health of farmers, farmworkers, or consumers. Managing cover crops for weed control rather than using herbicides in olive orchards is an example.

- When materials must be added to the system, use naturally occurring materials, such as compost for fertilizer, instead of synthetic, manufactured inputs.

- "Manage" pests, diseases, and weeds instead of "controlling" them.

- Reestablish the biological relationships that can occur naturally on the farm instead of reducing and simplifying them. For example, diversify the farm landscape to attract and maintain natural control agents of the olive fruit fly can occur.

- Make more appropriate matches between crop types and management that meet the productive potential and physical limitations of the local farm landscape. Olives might do best when they are integrated into a landscape that is already an open woodland ecosystem.

- Adapt the biological and genetic potential of agricultural plant and animal species to the ecological conditions of the farm rather than modifying the farm to meet the needs of the crops and animals.

- Value most highly the overall health of the agroecosystem rather than the outcome of a particular crop system or season.

- Emphasize conservation of soil, water, energy, and biological resources. Organic olives can promote a whole-systems approach to farming.

- Incorporate the idea of long-term sustainability into overall olive agroecosystem design and management.

The integration of these principles creates a synergism of interactions and relationships on an organic olive farm that eventually leads to the development of the properties of sustainable agroecosystems. Emphasis on particular principles will vary depending on where the organic olive farm is located, the scale of production, and the particular market focus of the farm operation, but all of these principles can contribute greatly to the conversion process.

For many farmers, rapid conversion to organic farming is neither possible nor practical. Regulations require a 3-year transition period, but for the reestablishment of many ecological processes and relationships, even this may not be enough. The soil system, for example, has to go through a period of development and adjustment after many years of conventional inputs and cultivation practices. As a result, many conversion efforts proceed in slower steps toward the ultimate goal of sustainability, and meanwhile make the initial changes necessary to meet organic standards. Studies on the organic conversion process are still very limited (see Swezey et al. 1994 and 1999; Hendricks 1995; Gliessman et al. 1996). They tell us that a lot of research still needs to be done not only to meet organic standards and improve yields and pest management, but also to improve the indicators of sustainability. Current research efforts point out three distinct levels of conversion, which are discussed below. These levels help us describe the steps that farmers actually take in converting from conventional agroecosystems, and they can serve as a map outlining a step-wise, evolutionary conversion process organic olive systems should take in order to ultimately achieve sustainability. They are also helpful for categorizing agricultural research as it relates to conversion.

Level 1: Increase the efficiency of conventional practices in order to reduce the use and consumption of costly, scarce, or environmentally damaging inputs

This approach is what we might call "pre-organic." Its goal is to use conventional inputs more efficiently so that fewer or different inputs will be needed and the negative impacts of their use will be reduced as well. This approach has been the primary emphasis of much conventional agricultural research, through which numerous agricultural technologies and practices have been developed. Examples for olives might include optimal tree spacing and density, improved harvest machinery, olive fruit fly monitoring for improved pesticide application, improved timing of pruning, and improved irrigation management. Although these kinds of efforts reduce the negative impacts of conventional agriculture, they do not help break its dependence on purchased inputs from outside the system, and they do not qualify for organic certification.

Level 2: Substitute conventional inputs and practices with organic practices

This approach can be called the "certified organic." The goal at this level of conversion is to replace resource-intensive and environment-degrading products and practices with those that are more environmentally benign in order to meet organic certification standards. Most organic farming research has emphasized this approach. Examples of alternative practices include the use of nitrogen-fixing cover crops in olive orchards to replace synthetic nitrogen fertilizers, the use of biological control agents for olive fruit fly control, and the shift to reduced or minimal tillage. At this level, the basic agroecosystem structure is not greatly altered; hence many of the same problems that occur in conventional systems, such as pest presence, weed infestation, and fertility loss, also occur in those with input substitution (see plate 6.6). Additionally, farmers must deal with the fact that many of these substituted inputs are as costly, if not more so, than conventional inputs.

Level 3: Redesign the agroecosystem so that it functions on the basis of a new set of ecological processes

The final level in the conversion process goes beyond organic certification, and can be called "sustainable organic." At this level, overall system design eliminates the root causes of many of the problems that still exist at levels 1 and 2. The goal becomes preventing the problems from arising in the first place. Whole-system conversion studies allow for an understanding of yield-limiting factors in the context of agroecosystem structure and function. Problems are recognized, and prevented, by internal site- and time-specific design and management approaches, instead of by the application of external inputs. An example from Andalucia, Spain, is the diversification of farm structure and management through the use of native plant diversity in the olive orchard understory; intercropping olives with other crops such as cereals, grapes, figs, and almonds; and the use of grazing animals such as sheep for weed management under the olive trees (Domínguez et al. 2002; Guzmán et al. 2000). Understory plants that are encouraged in the olive orchards attract beneficial insects, produce organic matter, recycle nutrients, and reduce erosion (plate 10.2).

In terms of research, agronomists and other agricultural researchers have done a good job of transitioning from level 1 to level 2 for olives, but the transition to level 3 has really only just begun. Agroecology provides the basis for this type of research, and eventually it will help us find answers to larger, more abstract questions, such as what sustainability is and how we will know we have achieved it (plate 10.3).

EVALUATING AND DOCUMENTING CONVERSION

As farmers undertake to convert their olives to organic management, it becomes important to develop systems for evaluating and documenting the success of these efforts and the changes they engender in the functioning of the agroecosystem. Such evaluation systems will help convince a larger segment of the agricultural community that conversion to sustainable organic practices is possible and economically feasible.

The study of the process of conversion begins with identifying a study site. This should be a functioning, on-farm, commercial olive production unit whose owner-operator wishes to convert to organic management and wants to participate in the design and management of the farm system during the conversion process (Swezey et al. 1994; Gliessman et al. 1996). Such a "farmer-first" approach is considered essential in the search for viable farming practices that eventually have the best chance of being adopted by other farmers.

The amount of time needed to complete the full ecological and agronomic conversion process beyond organic certification at level 2 depends greatly on the intensity of olive farming that has been going on, the local ecological conditions where the olives are located, and the prior history of management and input use. For short-term annual crops, the time frame might be as short as 3 years, but for a perennial crop like olives and animal systems, the time period is probably at least 5 years or longer. This would therefore be longer than the 3 years required for organic certification.

Study of the conversion process to full sustainability involves several levels of data collection and analysis.

- Examine the changes in ecological factors and processes over time through monitoring and sampling.

- Observe how yields change with changing practices, inputs, designs, and management.

- Understand the changes in energy use, labor, and profitability that accompany the above changes.

- Based on accumulated observations, identify key indicators of sustainability and continue to monitor them well into the future.

- Identify indicators that are "farmer-friendly" and that can be adapted to on-farm, farmer-based monitoring programs but are linked to our understanding of ecological sustainability.

- Develop economic indicators that balance market pressures with farm management strategies that take into account both short-term demands and long-term livelihood strategies, and link these indicators with on-farm ecological indicators.

Each season, research results, site-specific ecological factors, farmer skill and knowledge, and new techniques and practices can be examined to determine whether any modifications in management practices need to be made to overcome any identified yield-limiting factors. Ecological components of the sustainability of the system become identifiable at this time, and eventually they can be combined with an analysis of economic and social sustainability as well.

THINKING AHEAD

Converting an olive agroecosystem to organic management, as well as to sustainability in the broadest sense as defined above, is a complex process. It is not just the adoption of new practices, inputs, or technologies. There are no silver bullets. Instead, it uses the agroecological approach described above. The olive system is perceived as part of a larger system of interacting parts—an agroecosystem. Agroecology focuses on redesigning that system in order to promote the functioning of an entire range of different ecological processes (Gliessman 1998 and 2001). As the use of synthetic chemical inputs is reduced and eliminated and recycling is reemphasized, agroecosystem structure and function change as well. A range of processes and relationships begin to change, beginning with aspects of basic soil structure, organic matter content, and diversity and activity of soil biota. Major changes begin to occur in the activity of and relationships among weed, insect, and pathogen populations, and in the functioning of natural control mechanisms.

Ultimately, nutrient dynamics and cycling, energy use efficiency, and overall agroecosystem productivity are affected. Changes will likely be required in day-to-day management of the olive orchard, planning, marketing, and even philosophy. Olives can become part of a larger, more integrated landscape (plate 10.4). The specific needs of each olive orchard will vary, but the principles for conversion can serve as general guidelines for working our way through the transition. The agroecologist and the farmer must work together

to measure and monitor these changes during the conversion period in order to guide, adjust, and evaluate the conversion process. This approach provides an essential framework for determining the requirements for and indicators of sustainability.

ACKNOWLEDGMENT

This chapter is adapted from S. R. Gliessman, "Making the conversion to sustainable agroecosystems: Getting from here to there with agroecology," *California Certified Organic Growers Newsletter* 13:6–8 (2002). Its use as a basis for this chapter is gratefully acknowledged.

REFERENCES

Domínguez, A., J. Roselló, and J. Aguado. 2002. Diseño y manejo de la diversidad vegetal en agricultura ecológica. Valencia, Spain: Society for Ecological Agriculture.

ERS (USDA Economic Research Service). 2005. Organic production: The economics of food, farming, natural resources, and rural America. USDA Economic Research Service Web site, www.ers.usda.gov/data/organic/.

Gliessman, S. R. 1998. Agroecology: Ecological processes in sustainable agriculture. Boca Raton, FL: Lewis/CRC.

———. 2001. Agroecosystem sustainability: Towards practical strategies. Advances in Agroecology Series. Boca Raton, FL: CRC Press.

Gliessman, S. R., M. Werner, S. L. Swezey, E. Caswell, J. Cochran, and F. Rosado-May. 1996. Conversion to organic strawberry management changes ecological processes. California Agriculture 50:24–31.

Guzmán Casado, G. I., M. González de Molina, and E. Sevilla Guzmán. 2000. Introducción a la agroecología como desarrollo rural sostenible. Madríd: Mundi-Prensa.

Hendricks, L. C. 1995. Almond growers reduce pesticide use in Merced County field trials. California Agriculture 49:5–10.

Klonsky, K., and K. Richter. 2005. Statistical picture of California's organic agriculture. University of California Agricultural Issues Center Web site, http://aic.ucdavis.edu/research1/organic.html.

Swezey, S. L. and J. Broome. 2000. Growth predicted in biologically integrated and organic farming. California Agriculture 54:26–35.

Swezey, S. L., J. Rider, M. Werner, M. Buchanan, J. Allison, and S. R. Gliessman. 1994. Granny smith conversions to organic show early success. California Agriculture 48:36–44.

Swezey, S. L., P. Goldman, R. Jergens, and R. Vargas. 1999. Preliminary studies show yield and quality potential of organic cotton. California Agriculture 53:9–16.

11

Organic Certification and Registration in California

DAVID CHANEY, RAY GREEN, AND L. ANN THRUPP

BACKGROUND

The organic industry has grown significantly during the past 15 years. For the United States as a whole, the total market value (retail sales) of organic food products, including processed products, grew from about $1 billion in 1990 to an estimated $7.8 billion in 2000 (Dimitri and Greene 2002), while the Organic Trade Association estimated 2005 organic food sales at around $13.8 billion (OTA 2006). California producers have led this trend showing an increase in both numbers of organic farmers and total acreage. From 1992 to 2003, the number of registered organic farms in California grew by almost 30 percent, from 1,273 to 1,765 growers. Over the same period organic acreage quadrupled increasing from 42,000 acres in 1992 to almost 172,000 acres in 2003 (Klonsky and Tourte 1998, 2002; Klonsky and Richter 2005).

Prior to 1990, few common labeling standards were agreed upon and, for the most part, there was no regulatory requirement for certification. As the market began expanding, organic producers and marketers recognized the need for more uniformity and integrity in their products, and they turned to Congress for assistance in developing national standards. The result of these efforts was the Organic Foods Production Act (OFPA), which was passed in 1990 as part of the Food, Agriculture, Conservation, and Trade Act. OFPA mandated the U.S. Department of Agriculture (USDA) to establish an organic certification program for producers and handlers of agricultural products who sell and label their products as being organic. Responsibility for developing and administering a National Organic Program (NOP) was assigned to USDA's Agricultural Marketing Service (AMS). The intent of OFPA was to establish national practice standards governing the production and marketing of certain agricultural products as organically produced; to assure consumers that organically labeled foods represented these consistent standards; and to facilitate interstate commerce in fresh and processed food that is organically produced and labeled.

California had an organic labeling law in place from the 1970s, but it did not have any enforcement component. Concurrent with the development of OFPA, California passed its own law regulating organic farming, the California Organic Food Act (COFA), which was signed into law in 1990. COFA set a voluntary certification standard with full registration and enforcement components. Whereas COFA, the California law, became effective immediately upon signing, it took more than 10 years for the federal OFPA to be completed and implemented. COFA was eventually superseded by the federal regulations, and the law was rewritten to become the California Organic Products Act of 2003 (COPA).

The process of completing the national rule was complicated and controversial, involving numerous drafts and public input from consumers and the organic industry. USDA issued a proposed rule in 1997, but the final program was not completed until December 2000. The final rule states that all producers who gross more than $5,000 per year in retail sales must be certified through an accredited certification agency. These certifying organizations act as third-party agents of the NOP to legally verify that production and handling practices meet the national standards. Enforcement of the NOP began in October 2002, and AMS immediately began to accredit certification agencies to assist with its implementation.

In addition to accreditation of certifiers, the NOP ensures that the purposes of the OFPA are accomplished, determines the equivalency of foreign programs for imports into the United States, participates in development of international standards, coordinates enforcement activities with other agencies, conducts the petition process for materials review, and provides administrative support for the National Organic Standards Board (NOSB).

STATES AND THE NOP

States can serve two functions in relation to the NOP: they can choose to implement a State Organic Program (SOP), or they may become an accredited certifying agent, or they may do both. An SOP is primarily an enforcement program and is not involved in certifying growers or handlers. Once approved as an SOP, that agency is responsible for all aspects of enforcement within their state. A state agency that becomes an accredited certifying agent serves the same function of certifying organic production, processing, and handling as any other certification agency would. The list below provides examples of how three states are working in this area.

- California: The California Department of Food and Agriculture (CDFA) administers an SOP only; does not certify.

- Washington: The Washington State Department of Agriculture is an accredited certification agency only, not an SOP.

- Utah: The Department of Agriculture and Food administers an SOP and is also an accredited certifying agent.

In order to become an SOP, state-specific regulations or laws must be adopted that accept the standards set by the NOP. Upon approval by the USDA, state laws essentially become NOP laws for that state. COPA, for example, incorporates by reference the federal regulations and is interpreted in conjunction with them. Likewise, any future changes to the federal law automatically become regulations for California. Compliance and enforcement activities are contained within both the NOP and approved SOPs. Most states do not have an SOP and fall under the direct jurisdiction of the NOP in relation to enforcement activities. The NOP has a compliance and enforcement office based in Fresno, California, with two full-time staff. Their investigations are generally complaint-driven.

NOP IMPLEMENTATION IN CALIFORNIA

California's SOP is administered through the CDFA, which is responsible for raw agricultural commodities, meat, poultry, and dairy products; and the California Department of Health Services (DHS), which is responsible for processed food products, cosmetics, and pet food. The SOP's purpose is to protect producers, handlers, processors, retailers, and consumers of organic foods sold in California by enforcing labeling laws relating to organic claims for agricultural products. Its activities are coordinated with the California Organic Products Advisory Committee, the USDA, and the California county agricultural commissioners.

The California SOP's responsibilities include administering the program, training county biologists, investigating complaints, registering producers and certification organizations, and acting as a resource for information on COPA and the organic industry in California. The SOP is funded entirely by producer and certifier registration fees, a portion of which is used to support county enforcement activities. Because COPA unites the two separate statutes relating to fresh and processed products, it is important for individuals to read carefully the sections that relate to their type of business operation. (The text of COPA can be found at the CDFA Organic Program Web site, www.cdfa.ca.gov/is/fveqc/organic.htm.) For those involved in both growing and processing, they should note the specific requirements pertaining to each.

Producers

Organic producers and handlers (e.g., wholesale distributors, retailers, and some processors who market direct to retail or consumers) are regulated through the CDFA. In California, organic producers must become both registered and certified. All organic growers, regardless of gross sales, must be registered with the CDFA. In addition, any producer who grosses more than $5,000 per year in total sales must be certified through an accredited certification agency.

Registration is through your county agricultural commissioner and involves providing that office with a map of the production area, a list of crops that are intended to be produced as organic, and a 3-year history of substances or materials applied. Verification of land use history must be established, and an initial minimum registration fee of $75 is required. The actual registration fee is set according to the schedule shown in table 11.1. Fees for yearly renewal of registration follow this same schedule.

Certification is a separate process from registration. NOP regulations establish who must become certified in order to use the organic label on their products. The following general descriptions apply.

- Exempt from having to be certified: Producers who are grossing less than $5,000 per year in retail sales. Product must be produced, processed, and packaged under the producer's own label; product cannot be sold to anyone else for processing or packaging, although under the producer's own label the product can be marketed in retail stores.

- Excluded from requirement of having to be certified: Any operation or company that does not repackage or relabel the product (e.g., bulk wholesale distributor); or retail establishments that process or prepare organic product on the same premises at which they sell to the customer.

- Must be certified: All other operations involved in production, processing, and marketing.

If you are not sure whether you need to be certified or what category you fall into, contact the CDFA SOP office at (916) 445-2180. The steps involved in certification are described in more detail in the section "Certification Agents," below.

Processors

As defined in COPA, every person in California who processes, packages, stores, distributes, or handles processed food, pet food, or cosmetics in California that are sold as organic (except processed meat, fowl, or dairy products) is required to register with the DHS. Registration is handled through the DHS Organic Pro-

cessed Product Registration Program, and processors must pay an annual registration fee. As with producers, they must also be both registered and certified.

Registration of organic processors is directly through the DHS. The application is available by calling DHS or from their Web site, http://www.dhs.ca.gov/fdb/HTML/Food/organreq.htm. The application must be filled out completely and returned to the DHS with the appropriate fee. Upon receipt of the application and fee, the operation is registered, provided that they already possess a valid processed food registration permit from the DHS (this applies only if they are processing food for human consumption). There is no preinspection or verification; however, during the operation's regular food safety inspection, the inspector may ask questions about the organic aspects of the operation. The registration fee is set according to the schedule shown in table 11.2. Fees for yearly renewal of registration follow this same schedule.

It is possible that an operation or business must register both as producer and processor with both agencies (CDFA and DHS). For example, olive growers who also make and sell olive oil must be registered with both the CDFA and DHS. The registration fee for the CDFA is based on the market value of the olives prior to being processed; the fee for the DHS is based on the market value (gross sales) of the olive oil.

Certification is distinct from registration and involves the same steps and requirements for processors as it does for growers (see the section "Certification Agents," below). The same restrictions and exemptions described for producers also apply to processors. If a farming business is involved in both production and processing, it makes sense to find a certifying agency that is accredited to certify both aspects (production and processing) of the operation. Most certifiers do both, but it is wise to make sure.

Table 11.1. Fee schedule for companies required to be registered with the California Department of Food and Agriculture (CDFA)

Gross sales	Annual registration fee
$0–4,999	$ 25
$5,000–10,000	$ 50
$10,001–25,000	$ 75
$25,001–50,000	$ 100
$50,001–100,000	$ 175
$100,001–250,000	$ 300
$250,001–500,000	$ 450
$500,001–1,000,000	$ 750
$1,000,001–2,500,000	$ 1,000
$2,500,001–5,000,000	$ 1,500
$5,000,001–15,000,000	$ 2,000
$15,000,001–25,000,000	$ 2,500
$ 25,000,001–and above	$ 3,000

Note: Fees are subject to change; check with the CDFA for the most current fee schedule. Producers that sell processed product pay fees based on the value of raw product prior to being processed and the value of any product sold as unprocessed. Other exceptions are outlined in the text of COPA (see the CDFA Organic Program Web site, www.cdfa.ca.gov/is/fveqc/organic.htm).

Table 11.2. Fee schedule for companies required to be registered with the California Department of Health Services (DHS)

Gross annual sales or revenue	Annual registration fee
$0–$5,000	$ 50
$5,001–$50,000	$100
$50,001–$125,000	$200
$125,001–$250,000	$300
$250,001–$500,000	$400
$500,001–$1,500,000	$500
$1,500,001–$2,500,000	$600
$2,500,001 and above	$700

Note: Fees are subject to change; check with the DHS or CDFA for current fee schedule.

Some certifiers consider postharvest handling as a separate activity requiring a separate application, fee, and inspections. Other certifiers consider these activities as an addendum or attachment to the production side of the operation, which can be an advantage and reduce costs and paperwork for the grower. Any activities beyond simple postharvest handling would clearly fall under the "processing" rules and require separate registration and certification for each component.

If you are not sure whether you need to be certified or what category you fall into, contact the DHS Organic Processed Product Registration Program at (916) 650-6500. The remainder of this chapter, covering the certification process, is written mainly for growers, but the general principles and steps involved in becoming certified are applicable to processors as well.

THE ROLE OF ORGANIC CERTIFICATION AGENCIES

Producers should select the certification agency that will best serve their needs and budget (see sidebar 11.1). There are currently over 90 accredited certification agents approved by the USDA, including state and international agencies as well as private companies; about 20 of those are registered under the California SOP. All certifiers who want to operate in California must register with CDFA. An application fee is required from most certifiers, as are inspection fees. These are substantial, starting at around $500. If the operation intends to export their organic products out of the United States, they also need to have certification from the certifying body in the foreign country or from the International Federation of Organic Agricultural Movements (IFOAM). Some certifiers accredited through the NOP have direct partnerships with those foreign certifiers, meaning that they are accredited by those international agents and can verify certification for them.

The certifying agency monitors grower practices to assure that the grower is in compliance with NOP regulations. The certifier

- must know and enforce the NOP standards

- must verify producers' compliance with national standards through annual scheduled inspections of their clients' records, fields, and production and handling areas

- may perform annual soil and tissue tests from clients' operations in accordance with NOP guidelines

- may perform a certain number of surprise inspections per year

- must conduct ongoing review and inspection of clients' operations to ensure compliance

As a third-party agent of the NOP, the certifier is forbidden to provide advice on the operation, but it can and must provide information to the producer about the certification process and the legal requirements for maintaining certification. This means the certifier should know the client's operation in detail and have current knowledge of NOP regulations, but they may not act as a consultant to the grower. Certification agents must maintain their accreditation through the NOP and, as referred to in sidebar 11.1, may also become certification agents for foreign or international bodies. Some certifiers may also have a broader role in organic trade associations or in dealing with policy issues.

THE ORGANIC SYSTEM PLAN AND GROWERS' RESPONSIBILITIES

Growers should recognize that they also have responsibilities and commitments in relation to certification. According to NOP regulations, every certified organic producer is required to develop and keep current a production or handling system plan (OSP) that describes the operation and the practices and procedures to be maintained and also provides a list of each substance to be used as a production or handling input. The OSP includes

- land history

- sources of all seed and planting stocks used by the organic operation

- all inputs to the crop and all materials applied to the crop

- list of all practices and procedures for soil and pest management, fertility, and crop nutrition that are used in the operation, including details on monitoring practices

Sidebar 11.1
How to evaluate and select a certifier

Questions to ask yourself before you begin contacting certifying agents

- Will my product be sold only within California? If so, you may want to contact only agents with home offices in California. If the product will be sold outside California, other certifiers including those based in other states can be considered.
- Will my product be sold outside the United States? If not, you need only NOP certification. If you are exporting to other countries, then you should search for agents that certify according to international standards, such as the Japanese Agricultural Standard (JAS), the European Union (EU), or the International Federation of Organic Agriculture Movements (IFOAM), and who have knowledge of those markets.
- Is my "product" a raw crop or a processed food? Which agents seem to be strongest and provide the best service in relation to my final product? Do some research on the certifiers being considered.
- Who certifies my friends, and other companies like mine in the county or state? Talk to those companies and find out how satisfied they are with their certifying agent.

Questions to ask certifying agents after you have checked the NOP Web site and confirmed that the certifying agent is accredited by the NOP

- Given the products, land, or processing that I propose to certify, what are the expected costs for the initial submission of a certification request, actual certification on the first inspection, and expected ongoing annual costs? When are the fees due and payable?
- Is your cost or fee structure linked to organic sales, overall sales, number of acres, or complexity of the operation?
- Once paid, are any of my fees refundable if I decide to withdraw from application or from certification? Are there any additional costs or hidden fees?
- Are there any discounts for renewal clients?
- How many pages would a typical application package be for an operation similar to mine?
- I am going to export to a foreign country [give name of country or markets]. What is your expertise in certifying for this target market? What documents or transaction forms are required for export of organic product to this country? Are there any fees for generation of specific documentation required for each individual shipment?
- What are your policies regarding confidentiality of information and records?
- What are the charges if I need to add or change something (land, crop, product, SKU of same product, etc.) during the year and what documentation is required?
- Do you offer training programs in any aspect of organic compliance?
- Will you assist in any manner in marketing organic commodities?
- Do you have a Web site listing the companies you have certified? Do you list companies you have certified by commodity?
- Do you certify cohandlers under my application? In that situation, is the fee reduced?
- How long have you been certifying organic operations?
- What type of verification is needed to prove land history?
- How do you determine allowed and prohibited materials?

Other considerations

All certifiers are private companies or are a part of a government entity. Each has a different ability to respond to you and to provide services. Check the level of service by finding out:

- What is the average time that it takes the certification agency to complete a certification?
- What is the average time that it takes the agent to call back or respond to a question you may have?
- Do they provide supporting information that helps you understand compliance issues?
- What kind of support does the certifier offer for helping you understand and complete paperwork?
- Does the certifier provide a detailed explanation outlining the sections of the NOP that backup their certification positions and decisions?
- Are the inspectors friendly and courteous? Are the inspectors part of the certifying company or do they contract with independent inspectors? Do you have the option of choosing your inspector?

Notes

The NOP's official list of accredited certification agencies is published on its Web site at http://www.ams.usda.gov/nop/CertifyingAgents/Accredited.html.

The New Farm's Guide to U.S. Organic Certifiers is a very useful tool for learning about and comparing accredited certification agencies in the United States. For more information visit the New Farm Web site, http://www.newfarm.org/ocdbt/.

- explanation of barriers or buffers used to prevent commingling between organic and nonorganic products

- harvest and post harvest practices, including equipment use

- a description of records kept to prove compliance

- any additional information needed to document NOP compliance

Most certifiers provide a form that growers can use to prepare their OSP. These forms may be helpful for some growers, but they are not required; it's possible to write your own OSP. In either case, writing the OSP is useful for planning your farming operations for the year. Some certifiers may provide assistance in preparation of the OSP. The length of time to complete an OSP depends on the level of complexity of the farming operation.

The OSP is central to the certification process. It serves as a management tool to help farmers make decisions and react to changing circumstances. It also describes the human and natural resources of a farm, helps a producer manage those resources in an integrated way, and can assist the grower in budgeting and financial planning. Last, and most important, the OSP constitutes a legally binding contract between the certifier and the certified operation. Breach of that contract can result in denial or loss of certification. This last point is crucial, and growers must understand that the records they keep constitute the only proof that their "contract" (the OSP) has been fulfilled. The OSP is the commitment or promise to the certifier that production and handling will be carried out in a certain way, but the grower must show through good record keeping how he or she has kept that promise. Growers must get approval from their certifier if they are going to deviate from their submitted Organic System Plan.

In summary, the federal OFPA is a performance regulation, not a prescriptive regulation. This means the producer decides how they will grow or process their product and how they will demonstrate compliance with the NOP. The OSP is the individual grower's or operator's specific plan on how they are going to meet those performance targets. Growers should be proactive and create the roadmap for achieving compliance that works best.

THE TRANSITION AND STEPS FOR ORGANIC CERTIFICATION

The Transition Period

In order to be certified organic, it is required that the site not have any prohibited substances applied to it for 36 months. This can be accomplished if the site is not farmed (either historically or intentionally). If the site is actively being farmed, the grower must ensure (and verify with accurate records) that no synthetic, noncompliant materials were used during the 3-year period. During the transition, growers must educate themselves about the NOP and certification requirements (see the list of resources at the end of this chapter). Upon obtaining certification, the grower must implement all production practices addressed in the regulation and be proactive in building up soil organic matter with compost, cover crops, or other amendments; using organically acceptable methods for controlling weeds, insects, diseases, and any other pests; and implementing biodiversity. The grower must document in detail the names and amounts of every material they apply and must keep their OSP current. A producer does not need to be certified or registered during the transition period. For more information on making the transition to organic production, see chapter 10.

Keeping Records from the Start

It is very important for growers to keep careful records of the exact date the organic transition began, the last prohibited materials applied and when they were applied, and what specific inputs and practices are used during the 3-year period. When you apply for certification, the certifier will need to have detailed production practice records on those aspects. It is recommended to keep receipts and labels of organic inputs, and to get verification from neighbors, PCAs, county agricultural commissioner's pesticide use reports, or other local officials about when you ceased using prohibited pesticides and started the organic transition. Also, it is helpful to keep records of production activities or tasks by recording work orders or other labor records.

Contacting the Certifier

The certifier will send application materials to the grower. Certifiers expect growers to read the handbooks or literature they provide. The grower's OSP must be fully prepared and submitted with the forms as described below. Many certifiers require that growers sign an affidavit that shows land use history and affirms the truthfulness of the application. It usually takes 2 to 5 months for the application to be reviewed. Certifiers charge certification fees, which generally include

- one-time application fee (ranging from $100 to $300)

- inspection costs, which usually pay for an inspector's time to travel and inspect usually once per year

- annual fees (some use a fee based on acreage; others have an annual fee of some percentage of the gross production value)

The specific fees charged by each certifier should be given on their Web sites or by phone before a grower applies. The application fee must be paid when the application is submitted. The fees are charged in order to cover the costs of the certification procedures and to pay for the inspection staff. By paying the fees, growers gain the value of having the verification and credibility of being officially certified organic.

Review of Application, Inspection, and Notification of Certification

The certifier will review the grower's application and inspect the operation before certification is approved. A trained inspector calls the grower to set up the first inspection. After the inspection, the inspector submits a report to the certifier for review. The certifier informs the grower of the certification status or informs the grower of any requirements needed to achieve certification.

During an inspection, the inspector will want to review or see records about

- land use history

- pesticide use reports

- demonstration of cleaning or cleanout procedures if you use shared equipment

- demonstration that you understand the regulations (e.g., have read the appropriate manuals)

- the use of approved materials only

- demonstration of appropriate systems to ensure compliance

- product labels for products or inputs that you use

Annual Review and Inspection

Organic certification inspections are done on farms once per year, as required by the NOP. The inspector generally informs the grower of each visit in advance and sets up an appointment. However, certifiers and state organic inspectors have the right to make unannounced visits or inspections as well. If violations or problems are encountered by an inspector, the grower receives from the certifier a notice of minor noncompliance or major noncompliance. If the noncompliance is minor, the grower is reprimanded and told not to repeat the error, and may be sent a reminder about the particular issue. If the noncompliance is considered to be major, the growers' certification status may be affected. The grower may be required to submit requested documents or update a section of the OSP, or the grower can be decertified in serious cases.

As discussed previously, certification inspectors are not allowed to provide advice or information to the growers while doing inspections. They do not serve as consultants or advisors. This is intended to ensure that the role of the certifier is for enforcement and compliance. However, some certification agencies have departments or divisions that do provide information or educational materials to all growers, separate from the certification enforcement. In addition, many organizations, services, advisors, Web sites, and other resources provide information about organic practices.

Issues Regarding Compliant and Noncompliant Materials

All materials that can be used in crop and livestock production are classified into four categories under the NOP. Note that in the context of the NOP regulation, the words "nonsynthetic" and "natural" are used synonymously.

1. Allowed nonsynthetic. Most nonsynthetic (natural) materials are allowed except those specifically prohibited (category 2 below). There is not a list of allowed natural materials; the rule of thumb is, natural materials are allowed unless they are specifically prohibited.

2. Prohibited nonsynthetic. A few nonsynthetic (natural) materials such as arsenic and strychnine are not allowed under the NOP. See NOP Rule §§ 205.602 and 205.604.

3. Allowed synthetic. These synthetics are allowed, but their use is restricted for specific purposes as defined in the NOP Regulation and National List. Use of these materials for other purposes would be prohibited. See NOP Rule §§ 205.601 and 205.603.

4. Prohibited synthetic. Most synthetic materials are not allowed except those specifically approved for use in organic production (category 3 above).

The National List of allowed materials for organic production is overseen and maintained by the NOP (see the NOP Web site, http://www.ams.usda.gov/nop/NationalList/ListHome.html). The National List indicates generic compounds and materials that are allowed; it does not list specific brand name products. This information is available through the Washington State Department of Agriculture (see the WSDA Web site, http://agr.wa.gov/FoodAnimal/Organic/MaterialsLists.htm) and through the Organic Materials Review Institute (OMRI). OMRI is a private, nonprofit organization that provides verification and listings of products that meet the national organic standards. They publish two lists, a brand name list and a generic list, which are regularly updated. For more information visit the OMRI Web site, www.omri.org.

Certified growers are expected to keep track of updates and changes in the approval status of materials they use. Before trying new materials, growers should research the NOP, OMRI, and WSDA lists to make sure that the materials are allowed, and also get permission from their certifier to amend their OSP and use the product. Do not rely on the verbal or written declarations of vendors only. Confirm from other reliable sources any vendor claims.

The certification agency has the final decision on the acceptability of inputs for each farm operation. In making determinations about the acceptability of inputs, the certification agency must evaluate the input based on both the ingredients and the context in which the material will be applied. Prior to using any input on an organic farm the grower must obtain written approval (e.g., certificate of compliance) from the certifier. The certifier will contact the farmer and/or the manufacturer if additional information is needed to determine compliance of the material. As a word of caution, any input used by the farming operation without the written approval of the certifier could be viewed as a departure from the agreed-upon OSP and

could be grounds for adverse action by the certifier, the USDA, or state programs.

A summary of the certification process and the interaction between the grower and the certifier is outlined in table 11.3.

....

CERTIFICATION ISSUES FOR ORGANIC OLIVE OIL GROWERS AND PRODUCERS

Olive growers and processors who wish to use the label "organic" for their product must be certified according to NOP regulations. To use the organic label, an olive oil producer must use olives that are certified organic and must follow NOP regulations in processing the olives for oil. As indicated previously, if you grow and process olives, both aspects of your operation need to be certified and must be inspected yearly by an accredited certifier.

The goal of any organic processor is to maintain the organic integrity of the product. Some of the critical points that oil producers may want to address in the organic handling plan for their operation include the following.

Sanitation

When sanitizing equipment that comes in contact with organic product, the sanitizer must be in compliance with NOP. Prior to use, the sanitizer should be approved by your certifier. This approval also must be documented and recorded.

Cleaning

Normally, cleaning is required only if equipment has been contaminated with a prohibited substance. The cleaning method must assure complete removal of the prohibited substance, which may involve simple rinsing with cold water or several high-pressure hot water rinses, depending on the prohibited substance in question. Cleaning between organic and conventional fruit is not required inside continuous flow systems, but some of the first oil emerging from the organic fruit will have to be sacrificed as conventional until it is assured that there is no remaining conventional fruit, paste, or oil in the system to mix with the newly emerging organic oil. Bins should be rinsed out and the same wash water should not be used for organic fruit following conventional fruit.

Table 11.3. Roles and responsibilities of growers and certifiers

Grower	Certifier
Transition	
Read and understand NOP regulations. Gather information. Do research and planning. Begin transition.	
Document practices and management for 3 years. Select accredited certification agent.	Certifier would have a role only if grower seeks transitional certification.
Request application materials and instructions from certifier.	Provide materials and information to client (e.g., NOP regulations, application materials, etc.).
After 3 years	
Register with CDFA prior to sale of organic products.	Certifier not involved in registration—grower registers through CDFA.
Submit application and organic system plan for certification to certifier. This should be done well in advance of first anticipated organic harvest (6 months to 1 year).	Verify that grower is registered with CDFA and review application for certification in timely manner. Request additional information as necessary from grower.
Supply any new information or details requested by certifier to demonstrate compliance. Grower must submit to onsite inspection.	Conduct inspection and notify grower of results. Upon approval, OSP becomes legally binding contract.
Implement OSP. Record practices and procedures. Obtain prior approval for any alterations to the OSP. Keep accurate and detailed records. Keep records organized in preparation for annual inspection.	Annually review and inspect grower for assurance of certification compliance.

Tagging and Tracking

All certified organic olives coming into the processing facility must be specifically tagged, identified, and tracked to ensure that they are separated from other olives that are not organic.

Processing aids

Growers should consult the NOP list in § 205.605 for substances allowed as ingredients in or on processed products. Also check with your certifier before using any processing aid to determine compliance of the material.

Water

Water must be potable. Chlorine materials are allowed except that residual chlorine levels in the water should not exceed the residual disinfectant limit under the Safe Drinking Water Act.

Quality control

Consider doing a periodic assessment of the organic critical control points in the operation (e.g., transport trailers, washing devices, pressing equipment). The key questions to ask are: Where might the product lose its identity? Where could there be cross-contamination with nonorganic product?

Labeling for olive oil

Olive oil may be labeled as 100 percent organic if the olives used are certified organic and if all processing inputs and processes are in compliance with the NOP. If any nonorganic ingredients are added, the product may still be labeled as "organic" as long as the nonorganic ingredients constitute less than 5 percent of the final processed product. In both cases, the USDA organic label may be used, but it is not required.

. . . .

REFERENCES

Dimitri, C., and C. Greene. 2002. Recent growth patterns in the U.S. organic foods market. USDA Economic Research Service Publication AIB-777. ERS Web site, http://www .ers.usda.gov/Publications/aib777/.

Klonsky, K., and K. Richter. 2005. A statistical picture of California's organic agriculture: 1998–2003. University of California Agricultural Issues Center Web site, http:// aic.ucdavis.edu/research1/organic.html.

Klonsky, K., and L. Tourte. 1998. Statistical review of California's organic agriculture: 1992–1995. University of California Agricultural Issues Center Statistical Brief No. 6 (May). UC AIC Web site, http://aic.ucdavis.edu/ research1/organic.html.

———. 2002. Statistical review of California's organic agriculture: 1995–1998. Oakland: University of California Agriculture and Natural Resources Publication 3425. UC AIC Web site, http://aic.ucdavis.edu/research1/ organic.html.

OTA (Organic Trade Association). 2006. OTA's 2006 manufacturer survey. Summary at the OTA Web site, http:// www.ota.com/pics/documentsshort%20overview%20M MS.pdf

. . . .

INTERNET RESOURCES

ATTRA (National Sustainable Agriculture Information Service), http://attra.ncat.org/organic.html.

California Organic Program (Processors), http://www.dhs .ca.gov/fdb/HTML/Food/organreq.htm.

California Organic Program (Producers and processors), http://www.cdfa.ca.gov/is/fveqc/organic.htm.

Organic Farming Compliance Online Handbook, http:// www.sarep.ucdavis.edu/organic/complianceguide/.

OrganicAgInfo (Scientific Congress on Organic Agricultural Research), http://www.organicaginfo.org/Organic Materials Review Institute, http://www.omri.org.

Washington State Department of Agriculture Organic Food Program, http://agr.wa.gov/FoodAnimal/Organic/ default.htm.

USDA National Organic Program, www.ams.usda.gov/nop/ indexNet.htm.

INDEX

Color Plates

Site, Varieties, and Production Systems for Organic Olives

Plate 1.1
Olive trees growing on a shallow, rocky site without irrigation.

Plate 1.2
Various olive varieties picked on the same day.

Plate 1.3
High-density olive trees on the North Coast of California.

Plate 1.4
Super-high-density olive trees in California's Central Valley.

Plate 1.5
Mature open-center olive tree.

· · · · · · · · · · · · · · · · ·

Economics of Olive Oil Production

Plate 2.1
Super-high-density orchard harvested with an over-the-row harvester.

International Olive Oil Council Trade Standard for Olive Oil

Plate 3.1
Olive pomace oil.

Plate 3.2
Official sensory methodology.

Plate 3.3
Rotten olives, if made into oil, create defective oil.

Plate 3.4
COOC-certified extra virgin olive oil seal.

5.1

5.2

5.3

5.4

Organic Olive Orchard Nutrition

Plate 5.1
Low levels of nitrogen can lead to pale yellow leaves and a lack of shoot growth.

Plate 5.2
Blood meal, a concentrated organic fertilizer.

Plate 5.3
Compost application to tree rows in a young olive orchard.

Plate 5.4
Potassium deficiency symptoms.

Plate 5.5
Boron deficiency
symptoms on olive fruit.
The pit protrudes
from the bottom of the
fruit as severity increases.

Plate 5.6
Boron deficiency
symptoms on olive
leaves.

Plate 5.7
Nontilled olive orchard
in Australia with mowed
middles. The clipping
mulch is thrown into
the tree rows to provide
additional nutrients to
the trees and to help
control weeds.

Monitoring and Organic Control of Olive Fruit Fly

Plate 6.1
Adult female olive fruit fly *(Bactrocera (Dacus) oleae)*.

Plate 6.2
Olive fruit fly larva.

Plate 6.3
Olive fruit fly damage. Note exit holes.

Plate 6.4
Yellow sticky panel.

Plate 6.5
McPhail trap.

Plate 6.6
OLIPE trap.

Plate 6.7
"Attract and kill" target device.

Plate 6.8
Applying Naturalyte.

Plate 6.9
Kaolin clay barrier spray applied to an olive tree.

Organic Management of Common Insects and Diseases of Olive

Plate 7.1
Olive knot.

Plate 7.2
Peacock spot.

Plate 7.3
Verticillium wilt symptoms.

Plate 7.4
Armillaria root rot.
Bark has been removed
to expose mycelial
plaques.

Plate 7.5
Phytophthora crown
and root rot. Roots and
crown are exposed to
show darkened crown
and roots.

Plate 7.6
Black scale.

Plate 7.7
Oleander scale on leaves
and twigs.

Plate 7.8
Olive scale on fruit (dark spots), also known as Parlatoria scale.

Plate 7.9
Adult female olive scale with the covering removed.

Organic Weed Management in Olive Orchards

Plate 8.1
Black plastic used as mulch.

Plate 8.2
Mow-and-throw mower.

Plate 8.3
Cultivation in the
middles.

Plate 8.4
In-row weed remover

Plate 8.5
Weeder geese.

Plate 8.6
Flamer.

Agricultural Use of Olive Oil Mill Wastes

Plate 9.1
Liquid olive oil mill waste surrounded by dry bulking agents.

Plate 9.2
Turning compost windrows in compliance with regulatory standards.

Plate 9.3
The goal: productive olive orchards and zero environmental contamination.

Agroecological Principles for Making the Conversion to Organic Olive Agroecosystems

Plate 10.1
Farmers must learn new skill sets during the transition to organic management, such as how to direct-seed cover crop into resident vegetation between olive trees.

Plate 10.2
Native plant species forming a diverse understory in an olive orchard in Spain.

10.1

10.2

Plate 10.3
A comparison of
conventional and
transitional organic
strawberry production
using conversion study
protocols in California.

Plate 10.4
Olives integrated into a
diverse landscape.

Printed in the USA
CPSIA information can be obtained
at www.ICGtesting.com
LVHW070722090824
787692LV00012B/125

9 781601 074409